The Sailor Spy vs. UCI

A Firsthand Account and Analysis of the Largest Occurrence of Unlawful Command Influence (UCI) in United States Military History

Darin G. Lopez

Dedication

Before all else, I want to thank God for granting me the will, protection, and power to persevere in telling my story. I firmly believe that without God, this would not have been possible.

This book is dedicated to the countless individuals who have been wrongfully accused, unjustly convicted, and betrayed by a system that is meant to uphold the principles of justice. May your stories be heard, your voices amplified, and your dignity restored.

To the families and loved ones who have endured the anguish of watching their loved ones suffer under the weight of false accusations, this is for you. Your unwavering support and steadfast belief in their innocence have been the bedrock upon which they have found the strength to persevere.

Finally, to the brave whistleblowers and advocates who have risked their careers and reputations to expose the systemic failures within the military justice system, this book is a tribute to your courageous actions. You have paved the way for a future where truth and accountability will reign supreme.

Acknowledgment

The journey of bringing this book to life has been challenging, deeply difficult, and an all too personal one. I owe a debt of gratitude to the many individuals who have supported me along the way. But this book doesn't start with just simple words on paper. It starts with living out this terribly painful journey that led to the book. There have been many great people I would love to acknowledge. And I know if you are reading this, you know who you are, so I will not mention some out of respect and for fear of any negative action or reprisal against you for your support.

First and foremost, I must express my heartfelt appreciation to my entire family, whose unwavering love and support have been the guiding light during the darkest moments of my life. To my parents, whose unyielding belief in my innocence and steadfast advocacy have been a constant source of strength, thank you. Your determination to see justice prevail has been an inspiration to me and countless others. As they say, one good rock thrown into the water makes many positive ripples. While they have been my rock, the encouragement and support I have received are overwhelmingly priceless as the opportunity for positive change ripples out into this world as a light for those living in darkness. So, while the book may help your journey, remember your journey is their journey as well. Never quit. Never give up.

To the mentors and advocates who have walked alongside me, offering guidance, wisdom, and a shoulder to lean on, I am forever grateful. Bruce Lockett, who has now been laid to rest, your selfless dedication to serving our veterans and your belief in the power of advocacy have left an indelible mark on my life. Congressman Randy Weber's office and his tireless assistants, your efforts to provide resources and support have been invaluable. Senator Ted Cruz, Governor Abbott, Allen West, and countless others in the political world, the opportunity to advocate, knowing that my interest is your interest, only reinforced my will to continue my plight, and for that, I am forever thankful.

I would also like to acknowledge the members of the Defense Advisory Committee on Investigations, Prosecutions, and Defense of Sexual Assault in the Armed Forces (DAC-IPAD) for granting me the opportunity to share my story and advocate for the creation of the Falsely Accused Individual Review (FAIR) unit. Your willingness to listen and consider the pressing need for reform has been a glimmer of hope in a landscape often shrouded in darkness.

To the brave whistleblowers who have risked their own careers to expose the insidious nature of Unlawful Command Influence, your actions have been a beacon of courage and a testament to the power of truth. Your stories have inspired me to continue fighting for the restoration of justice.

Finally, to the countless individuals, friends, friends of friends, fellow service members, and so many others, whether victims or supporting their loved ones, who have reached out to me, shared their own stories of struggle and offered words of encouragement, I am deeply grateful. Your resilience and determination have been a constant source of inspiration, reminding me that I am not alone in this fight.

Together, we will continue to raise our voices, demand accountability, and work tirelessly to transform a system that has for too long been tainted by the corrosive influence of injustice.

About the Author

Darin G. Lopez is a seasoned military intelligence professional with over a decade of experience serving the nation. Throughout his 12-year career, he underwent rigorous FBI background investigations, holding positions that required the highest levels of integrity and discretion. His expertise extends across multiple military branches, having trained with and supported the Navy, Army, Marine Corps, Air Force, Coast Guard, and their special forces, along with key government agencies and contractors.

During his service, Darin dedicated himself to protecting the rights of service members and veterans, even while facing his challenges. As a BRIG lawyer during his time in confinement, he successfully advocated for the rights of many fellow service members, spending 2.5 years studying case law.

In addition to his military credentials, Darin has pursued a diverse academic journey, earning an Associate Degree in Social Sciences, an Associate Degree in Applied Sciences with a focus on Intelligence Operations Studies, a Bachelor's in Business Administration (BBA) in Technology Management, and an MBA in Marketing. This multi-disciplinary education has helped him develop a unique perspective on human psychology, communication, and the overall broader world.

With his relentless pursuit of justice and a purpose-filled life, Darin remains committed to leaving the world better than he found it. His advocacy for Unlawful Command Influence and the Feres Doctrine changes stems from a deep-seated belief in fairness, transparency, and protecting Constitutional rights for all service members based on his experiences. He believes strongly in his plight and strives for an improved and just future for all.

Legal Disclaimer

This book is a work of non-fiction based on the personal experiences and recollections of the author, Darin Lopez. While every effort has been made to accurately portray the events described, some details may have been altered or fictionalized to protect the privacy of the individuals involved. The views and opinions expressed in this book are those of the author and do not necessarily reflect the official policy or position of any government, military, or other organization. The author has made a good faith effort to ensure the information presented is truthful and factual to the best of their knowledge.

This book is not intended to provide legal advice or to be used as a substitute for professional legal counsel. Readers are advised to seek the advice of a qualified attorney for any legal matters arising from the content of this book. The author and publisher disclaim any liability for loss or damage as a result of reliance on the information contained herein. Readers proceed with the understanding that they assume all risks associated with the use of this material.

This disclaimer aims to protect the author and publisher from liability related to the truthful but potentially sensitive nature of the events described in the book. It clarifies that some details may have been altered, the views expressed are the author's own, and that readers should seek professional legal advice if needed. The copyright notice also establishes the author's ownership of the work.

Preface

There's no greater power on this earth than story, and I've never got to tell my side.

I feel compelled to share this narrative because of the potential power of positive change I can unleash by telling my own side of this story. Stories have the unparalleled ability to connect people, evoke emotions, and drive positive change. In a world where injustice persists, even within the hallowed halls of our military, the power of storytelling becomes a clarion call for reform.

Throughout my life, I have been guided by the belief that if something matters, it is worth fighting for. As I reflect on the egregious violations of individual rights that I have endured, I know that my story must be told—not merely for the sake of personal redemption but for the sake of all those who have been wrongfully accused, unjustly convicted, and stripped of their dignity by a system that is meant to uphold the highest ideals of justice.

This book is a testament to the resilience of the human spirit, forged in the crucible of adversity. It is a chronicle of my journey through the darkest corners of the military justice system, where Unlawful Command Influence (UCI) reigned supreme, and the very foundations of due process were crumbling under the weight of political agendas and institutional biases.

But this is more than just my story. It is a rallying cry for those who have been silenced, a beacon of hope for those who have lost faith, and a call to action for all those who believe in the inviolable principles of fairness and accountability.

As you turn the pages of this book, I invite you to walk with me, to feel the weight of the injustice thrust upon me and countless others. Let the stories of courage, resilience, and the unwavering pursuit of truth inspire you to become a catalyst for change. Only through the collective power of our voices can we transform the very systems that have betrayed us.

The road ahead may be arduous, but I am steadfast in my belief that justice will prevail. With each word, paragraph, and chapter, I hope to ignite a fire within you—a fire that will burn brightly, illuminating the path toward a military justice system that truly upholds the values it is sworn to protect.

So, let us embark on this journey together for the sake of those who have been wronged and for future generations. May this story serve as a beacon, guiding us toward a future where the power of the pen and the courage of the heart can overcome the forces of injustice.

Contents

Introduction

Have you ever wondered why parents would tell their children stories and not bedtime facts when putting them to sleep? According to Libba Bray:

"There's no greater power on this earth than story."

Those words quoted by the great American writer of young adult novels and that concept of the story are something that has been ingrained in me ever since I was a young man. Understanding the power of the story, coupled with the fact that there are two sides to every story and only one side has been told, compels and empowers me to tell my story out of necessity.

Stories have long been utilized as powerful tools for communication, connecting people across time and technology. They evoke emotions, provide context, and drive social change by engaging individuals on multiple levels—mind, imagination, values, and emotions. By sharing narratives of the world we envision, we can shape societies and beliefs, avoiding past mistakes.

The essence of storytelling lies in its ability to convey meaning that resonates with audiences, fostering unity and sparking action. With the right storyteller and platform, stories can be used for virtuous causes, such as creating positive social change. They have the potential to connect people from all walks of life through shared experiences, building bridges, and overcoming differences.

Just as Libba Bray conveys the essence and power of the story, she also states:

"Write like it matters, and it will."

Well, here I am, world, writing like it matters because it does matter, and it will to those who need to read or share it. The scope and scale of how much it matters is arguably debatable. However, when I might be the sole person responsible for sharing the story that changes one's world, or the entire world for that matter, a person can realize, upon the review of draft after draft, that sometimes there may not be perfect words. But that's the power of intent. I have intended from the start, as I have promised myself, the others who I know have suffered injustice, for those still struggling that I may not ever know, and those who are no longer with us on this earth. I will do my best in hopes of pressing for positive change.

Stories can challenge self-limiting beliefs, empowering individuals to cultivate resilience and possibility. By shifting our internal dialogue from doubt to confidence, we can navigate challenges with determination. Just as The Little Engine that Could declared, "I think I can, I think I can," we too can embrace a mindset of belief in our abilities and potential for success. However, do not be misled; there is more than enough hard work to do between thinking and doing.

But faith without works is dead, so don't forget that as you travel your journey believing that you can achieve, there is a lot of work that needs to be done between those motivational self-affirmations.

Scientifically speaking, the best stories simplify the brain's process of storing data for later retrieval. The emotions they trigger signal the brain that whatever the person is experiencing is important. Therefore, the brain pays much more attention than it normally would and saves the acquired information that's charged with emotion in the deepest parts, such as the cerebellum. On top of that, if the story you read presents something you can highly relate to, there's a great chance that the information will take deep root in your memory. The emotional content of a story, in particular, greatly improves the odds that a reader will act on the information shared or that their life will be shaped somehow.

This power of storytelling can spark flint to create fire and light the hearts of troops to take charge against great opposition, for instance, by calling on the tales of the Spartan battle spirit.

If you recall, the "Spirit of the Spartan" tale taught us valuable lessons about rational thinking and action in our everyday lives. It inspired people to act rationally and think through an obstacle versus charging forward into their prideful demise, awaiting the ship to sink fully. Be bold, be brave, but don't be stupid.

The story emphasizes that sound decision-making requires a level head despite being faced with difficult circumstances. Spartans were renowned for their courage and tenacity in battle but knew when to retreat if the odds were too great. This principle is still applicable today in all aspects of life.

Alternatively, the story can be used to inspire an athlete to push themselves to surpass past limitations. Spartans were known for their relentless pursuit of physical perfection and the ability to endure pain. Even in the face of seemingly insurmountable obstacles, Spartans never gave up—an inspiring trait for modern-day athletes looking to break through their own barriers.

However, the irony is that different people will receive and embrace different messages from the same story. This may cause them to act in a completely opposing fashion. For example, one may think it is better to stick with the status quo and never take risks. The lesson here is to be aware of our bias when interpreting stories while still taking something positive from them. In just about every story, there is a golden nugget to store away that may come in handy one day.

Hence, the story has served as a double-edged sword—useful for inspiring and teaching us to think rationally and as a warning against rash decisions.

But at the same time, the story serves as a substance or source of inspiration that can't be described so literally. It isn't as straightforward as a math equation because the storytelling portion is artistic, even if it is based entirely on fact. It's up to the listener or reader to interpret it and decide how it might relate to them. This is what makes the Spirit of the Spartan story so powerful — it has universal relevance, no matter who you are or where you come from.

So, if you're overwhelmed by circumstances beyond your control, you can always pick up a book and count on its power to turn things around. Designed to do just that, this book deeply defines me and the obstacles I have faced and continue to face in my life. The layout was intended not just to have a voice to sound the alarm but also to build a bridge for me, offering insights into my character and who I am as a person.

This story, just about as well as any, has the power to enlighten minds. It's about me waging a war against injustice that has existed in the American military for ages. It's about all the fierce encounters I faced during my service in the US Navy and how I battled against the entire armed forces as well as the President in hopes of turning things around and reviving justice.

Providing deep insights into the reality of the military justice system of the country and how it actually works, this story is my attempt to show how it has been weaponized against its own soldiers. Despite all the obstacles that exist even today, I continue to relentlessly fight, expose, and work to correct the wrongdoings of these institutions. This book is a part of that effort, as much as it is a message to you to fight for the good, and as Churchill famously stated:

"Never give in, never give in, never, never, never, never-in nothing, great or small, large or petty – never give in except to convictions of honor and good sense."

Given the nature of my work and study in the Intelligence field, as I experienced the events of my story, I quickly realized I wasn't up against a person; I was up against an idea and an agenda. So, it was no wonder that I couldn't immediately foresee the consequences of my actions. The power of this idea was so strong that it had become a force in its own right. I must admit that I did have opportunities to alter the course that, in hindsight, I know would have led to a better outcome, which would have avoided the entire thing. But the thought-critical truth seeker in me would not allow stopping. I don't know if it was divine or my nature, but I had to see this thing through even when things felt very "off," to say the least.

I quickly discovered that I needed more than just strength and courage to fight this oppressive force; I needed strategy and resilience. I had to be willing to step out of my comfort zone and take calculated risks. It wasn't easy, but I knew that I had to be fearless if I wanted to know the truth, make a difference, and see real change.

I did and still do experience small victories that I refer to as my journey to redemption, but the path was not a straight one. Like the Good Book and Joel Osteen say, "from victory to victory," because I either win or learn; there is no loss or failure. Along the way, I encountered darkness and hopelessness that often threatened to derail my progress. But I kept going, believing in myself, staying in faith, and trusting that better days were ahead.

Through these pages, I will tell the unheard portion of my story that is only known to a few. It is meant to be informational as to who I am as a person, what injustice happened to me, exposing the largest injustice in military history from the inside out, and my journey to fight for change and, hopefully, my own redemption. I am writing to inspire others to fight for injustice while also pursuing their dreams and staying flexible to things that we cannot control. Unfortunately, for some, the individual rights we are supposed to be protected by in the Constitution are seen as optional. I hope and pray that those who hold this view may never have a seat in any political leadership position.

I strongly feel that my story will provide insight and encouragement to those struggling with similar issues. I will take you through the journey of how I overcame circumstances beyond my control, using positive thinking and determination as fuel for success and seeking what courses of action would have the most impact and could most easily be sold as win-win's.

Like many sensitive topics or taboo subjects, this story will provoke a broad range of emotions and likely even more opinions. However, regardless of how these words make you feel, or what opinions they lead you to form, my greatest hope is that my story sparks positive inspiration. You were born to accomplish great things in this life; don't let fear hold you back from achieving them.

"Helping one person. Might not change the world. But it could change the world for one person."

My story begins with a false accusation, but before I go further into that, let me share a quote from a seasoned 20+ year battle-tested Navy SEAL who admitted that he never experienced anything as difficult as being falsely accused. That fact alone should add some perspective to how devastating such a thing is. Here is what he said:

"It's like being in a fight you can't win. No matter what you do, it just keeps coming at you."

So, suppose one can survive this experience and become stronger and better equipped mentally and physically to face opposition or just life in the future. In that case, I'm confident anyone can do the same.

Unfortunately, problems like this will keep happening throughout life. Maybe not of this magnitude, but my greatest hope is that after you read my story, you will be prepared to go forth all the wiser, understanding what can happen and what you can do to help the effort. Learn how to keep bringing the good fight to any obstacle and continue to tell your own story to assist in safeguarding our futures. Keep in mind that small victories lead to bigger ones, and with bigger victories comes tougher opposition. At this time in the greater struggle for reform and rallying support for my plight, the culmination of our stories and support will ultimately drive the advance.

My story proves that even in the darkest times, we can find strength and courage to face our struggles. We just need to remember that no matter what, we cannot give up hope. With resilience, determination, and faith in ourselves, anything is possible. So don't be afraid to stand up for what's right; never forget the power of your voice, and always keep fighting for justice. I personally didn't recognize the power of having a voice in this world until it was taken from me.

Through resilience and determination, I eventually triumphed over this powerful force. It wasn't easy, but it was worth the struggle. Now, I look back on my story with pride: not only did I survive the oppressive force, but I also managed to make a difference. My story has inspired many and motivates me to continue fighting for what's right.

Ultimately, I learned that no force is too powerful; anything can be accomplished with courage, resilience, and determination. No matter how dark the situation may seem, there is always hope and strength to be found within. It is never too late to make a difference, no matter how daunting the task ahead might seem; all we need is courage and the willpower to persevere.

Throughout these pages, you will understand how strength and resilience can be found even in the most dire situations. You will gain insight into transforming negative thinking into positive thought patterns and learn the importance of facing life's challenges with courage and determination. I hope my story will inspire you to tap into the strength within yourself and strive toward a brighter future.

My greatest wish is that whosoever reads this book closes it with a mind capable of pursuing their dreams in the face of opposition and fighting relentlessly against injustice. I hope it will provide guidance and solace to people in need and that all readers can find the power to make each day better, no matter how difficult.

This book is written with love, understanding, and respect. As you read this story, I want you to remember that adversity may seem insurmountable, but it is completely possible to turn things around. You can and will prevail if you have faith in yourself and never give up. But if you must panic, do it fast, get over it and get back to work. As my medical school professor used to tell our class, "If you don't know "how" to limit panic, do a search for box breathing." This is what they teach us in special forces to maintain stressful times.

By sharing this narrative, I wish to instill unwavering faith in those who read or hear my story. No matter the obstacles, odds, or how hopeless it may seem, remember that you are capable of greatness. I feel honored to be a part of your journey to success. This book also seeks to actively convey that maintaining what I call a victory mindset is essential for success.

But what exactly is this?

It's a way of thinking and focusing on your goals that gives you the self-confidence and motivation to achieve them.

This kind of mindset tends to strive for excellence, expecting success in all things undertaken. With this attitude, you focus on what can be achieved instead of dwelling on past failures or setbacks. You take risks, approach challenging tasks enthusiastically and optimistically, and work to achieve the best possible outcome. Doing so creates a strong foundation for self-belief and motivation that can help you reach even greater heights of success at any stage of your life.

A success-oriented mindset emphasizes self-reflection and learning from mistakes to gain knowledge and improve your performance over time. By reading this book, you can develop that mindset to help you succeed in any endeavor.

Through this approach, you can cultivate resilience and foster a more positive outlook on life. You'll become better equipped to handle difficult situations and use opportunities when they arise. Additionally, a more positive outlook can help you to stay focused on your goals and maintain momentum toward achieving them. The mindset will also set an example for others and encourage positivity around you. Keep in mind that the victories will not always be yours; instead, you will be helping others achieve successes of their own because you will be equipped with knowledge and understanding. The dormant leader in you will grow just as the tree grows with the bent limb.

A victory mindset is a mindset of vision, personal accountability, and reorientation applied to everything you do. Let me shed some more light on this. A success-oriented mindset means being willing to look honestly at yourself and embracing the possibility of making changes. It encourages you to proactively seek opportunities and challenges that will help you reach your goals and break through the barriers.

It is also about recognizing that failure is not a dead-end but a learning opportunity and a chance to realign your focus. John Maxwell, a renowned leadership figure, motivational speaker, and pastor, once said:

"Fail early, fail often, but always fail forward."

Successful individuals grasp that adaptability is key to achieving success. A proactive mindset enables individuals to remain upbeat and driven in challenging times, acknowledging that every setback offers a new chance to triumph.

Fostering a proactive mindset entails appreciating the journey and the lessons it provides. Celebrating victories and reflecting on mistakes and challenges are vital components of personal development. This mindset promotes growth by encouraging individuals to take risks, challenge themselves, and make decisions in a transparent and honest manner through self-assessment. By maintaining mindfulness about your thoughts and beliefs, you create an environment conducive to success in any circumstance. A proactive mindset unlocks potential and propels individuals toward attaining their goals.

As you embrace a victory mindset, it's critical not to lose sight of your vision, as having a clear goal ensures progress. Striving with confidence and perseverance is essential to realizing dreams, as achievements require active participation. Believing in your capabilities, staying focused, and persisting through challenges are fundamental to pursuing and achieving your aspirations. Even when you face difficulties, digging deep and pushing past the halfway mark can create the momentum you need to move forward toward success. Once you're halfway there and take at least one more step, you're closer to the finish than you were at the start.

When you experience moments of triumph, use them as motivation to keep going, and remember to express gratitude for your accomplishments. With a positive mindset, the possibilities are limitless. Courage and a commitment to excellence are prerequisites for success in all aspects of life. Embracing change and striving for excellence in every endeavor signifies the pursuit of meaningful goals.

So yes, this story has the power to help you. By the end of this book, I hope that readers will have acquired a new, more positive outlook on life and will be ready to start their journey to improvement.

Good luck on your path to redemption! May you find the strength within yourself that will help you prevail against the odds.

Chapter 1: Growing and Learning

"When something is important enough, you do it even if the odds are not in your favor."

That quote from Elon Musk pretty much sums up my life's mantra, which was revealed early in my life and followed through during my adolescence years, high school life, and thereafter, getting me here, even before I knew who Elon Musk was.

What it means is that if doing or achieving something is genuinely important to you, you'll go on to pursue it without giving much thought about how things will really work out. If it's something that matters to you, you'll deliver your best to make it happen, even if the odds are against you or the chances of success seem low. There's also a great chance that the only thing that will be on your mind is to accomplish that goal, and when this does happen, nothing and no one can stop you from making that dream a reality.

Throughout my elementary, intermediate, and middle school years, I had been a very involved young man who would actively participate in sports and extracurricular activities, playing in the woods, making bike tracks, learning to play guitar, climbing and making tree obstacle courses, and shooting guns in the country. I also volunteered in choir activities such as singing in Christmas concerts and role plays. This led me to perform a solo song I wrote, playing my guitar in the auditorium in front of several classes. As far as role plays are concerned, I still remember taking part in a play in which I showed up in a black top hat, beard, and sideburns to enlighten everyone about Gettysburg, which is known for the Gettysburg National Battlefield, the famous site of a turning point in the Civil War, and that marks the site of Abraham Lincoln's 1863 Gettysburg Address. Yes, I got the privilege to represent the "Honest Abe," that is, Abraham Lincoln.

Academically, I was a decently "outstanding" student who would finish my class work earlier than most and take naps or pass notes to my fellow classmates to spark conversations. But at the same time, like any other intelligent person, I was a suck-up to most of my teachers, which worked to keep me out of trouble and in good graces. I also mentioned that I was in honors classes, which offered more in-depth insights and covered more challenging material. These classes required extra time and effort for projects and tests that were tougher than standard ones. So again, hard work and reinforcement were the keys that set me apart from many of my peers. In mathematics, for example. Some students had a natural talent for it, while I had strengths in other areas. For math, I didn't have that same natural ability, so I had to work hard and practice a lot just to keep up with those early geniuses academically.

Outside the class, I participated in every sport that I was exposed to. Other than a game, our Physical Education (PE) Coach called Four Square Tag, where our fastest runners, such as myself, would shine, and baseball was the earliest sport in which I would outplay my peers. In the Junior

League, I would hit so many home runs and was such an incredible hitter that, on many occasions, coaches had to pause the game to have the umpire check my bat as if my performance had something to do with it. The secret to my extraordinary hitting was that I had been gifted a batting practice machine that I made the most out of. Looking back, I realized that repetition was a major key to success. While I was way above average than most kids in the league, baseball soon became boring for me, and I didn't play more than a few more seasons. I was in search of a harder sport, and baseball certainly wasn't one of them. Even later in life, my younger brother would challenge me in batting cages, which meant I wasn't totally done with it. But honestly, I was making nearly 100% contact and getting some great hits in a fast-pitch setting, which felt close to perfect—even though I hadn't held a bat in 20 years.

By middle school, I had lost interest in baseball and started engaging in football, basketball, tennis, track and field, as well as running. In the beginning, I failed to make it to the school basketball team because, as my coach put it, *I needed to get better*. This was enough of a compliment to challenge me, and I became determined to master it. I believe, for my height, I had gotten about as close as a person can.

At this time in my life, I discovered a strange trait in myself: I would get bored with activities I excelled in, and my focus would divert to newer ones, especially those I wasn't good at, or so the coach would say I would need some work to be competitive. Every time I found something challenging, I would dedicate all my extra time to performing better and better at it. Today, when I look back, I realize that if I had developed a plan, I could have easily earned scholarships by sticking with baseball since I was good at it and was "built" for it, as they say. I personally believe I could have easily made it to the Minor League or even the Pro League with the right support, but then again, I was following my ambitions, my desires, and, ultimately, my passions. But I'll stop dwelling on that; it's really up to you to choose your own paths in life. Even though those decisions brought me challenges that I thrived on, things would have been very different if I had gone down that route. I believe it would have been less exciting and more predictable, and I would have been content with my teams and earnings. But at the end of the day, that was not me and not for me. For all I know, I could have got benched for injury and never got to play, or worse, getting stuck on a practice team. Like I said, it was within my wheelhouse but not my passion.

It's just that excelling in baseball and sizing up the competition made me feel that I had had enough of the sport. It was time to move on to more exciting things because this was going to lose its shine fast. Thus, my lost interest and passion for baseball were attributed to the lack of challenge it posed for me.

However, sports weren't the end of the road for me. I discovered that playing the drums in the percussion instruments was a lot of fun, and my section had the coolest people to play with, so I joined the middle school band. Over time, I became skilled enough to be consistently positioned on the first and second chair, which, in layman's terms, meant the best and second best, respectively.

Learning to play various instruments was a challenge due to the skill required for each, but thanks to my drive, dedication, and private lessons, I was selected for the All-City Band, which hosted a festive Holiday Program every year. The highlight of my band career came in my 8th-grade year, right before high school, when my best friend and I tried out for the High School Marching Band. Competing against participants from many other schools, we ended up taking the 1st and 2nd chairs in the entire high school percussion section. Ask the band experts, and you'll find how big of a deal that achievement was in the world of the band. Again, this is not advice, but sticking to this path would have easily paid for all of my college tuition, but it wasn't my passion.

During my time in the band, I never gave up on sports and stayed on top of all the athletic activities mentioned earlier, as well as my academics. I was a go-getter, and that attitude only grew and refined over time. While I wasn't the finest player in football, my athletic nature meant I could play any position and do fairly well. Some of the positions I would play include backup quarterback, defensive end, tight end, and kicker, all of which require different skills. Not only could I kick decently, but my overall performance was impressive at a middle school athletics level. This is proved by the piles of ribbons, certificates, and trophies that I still have from 1st place down to 4th or 5th, which I earned in various competitions. Upon leaving that school, I even held the records for most wins and points earned in a single-track meet while also breaking the school's high jump record that remained unbeaten for many years.

Besides the high jump, I even competed and was somewhat successful in the long jump, javelin, shot put, and running events. On the running front, I didn't hesitate to cover the 400-meter relay, 100-yard dash, 300 hurdles, and 400-meter run. My drive to grow athletically earned me the male 'Athlete of the Year' award at the end of 8th grade, the year I graduated from middle school. An award only coveted by one person every year. In addition, I broke track records that earned me the "placing" for most awards, particularly in middle school and a little less in high school. Since I worked hard and earned that recognition, I felt proud of myself and stored all those memorable ribbons in what I call my "I love me" box, a term I picked up from my time in the Navy. No, this box was not a box of narcissism. It's a box of overcoming, a box of excellence, a box of accomplishments from all of the hard work, and a box of future motivation and inspiration to my future self to remember who I am.

Upon getting started with my high school, I noticed that it wasn't too different, except that the number of students was much higher. The immediate and greatest obstacle I faced in high school was the trend of dating and partying.

When everyone around you seems to be dating, and parties are held almost every weekend, it's easy to fall for the pleasures and lose track of your goals, especially at that age.

Since I had my standards and values, I was quick to track the hurdles and formulate a strategy to move forward. The plan was to avoid too many parties, seek out and have one girlfriend, and try my best to stay focused on personal growth, which was more difficult at the time than you think. I strictly adhered to these rules until my senior year, after which staying single made the most sense to me. I will say this, though, that I never had a lack of attention from the ladies, and that would be a blessing and a curse until I was mature enough to know how to entertain the attention correctly or leave it alone. Even though I had no idea where life would take me next, I was excited and enthusiastic.

Apart from that, one of the first major decisions I had to make upon transitioning into high school was to choose between football and band. Not only was my personal strength showing through in the band, making me one of the best performers among the freshmen, but it also positioned me at the top among all of the students, so again, I had great scholarship potential. On the other hand, athletics attracted me more, and I felt like I was built for them. From a very young age, I saw myself as an athlete, so I geared up for football, dropping my drums and drumsticks behind once and for all, but never my guitar.

While I actively played football during my freshman and sophomore years, I would often find myself practicing basketball somewhere almost every day. Since I was an ex-terrible basketball player and was improving, the game was more dynamic and still appeared to me as a challenge. As stated earlier, challenges would trigger a kind of supernatural energy within me, so I began exhibiting some remarkable improvements. Thanks to my impressive athleticism, I was looked to be on the team every year.

During my sophomore year, my coach advised me that to maintain a good position on the team, I should choose between basketball and football. By this time, my passion for basketball had far outgrown my craving for football, so I opted for the former. Compared to the earlier football-band tradeoff, this was a much easier decision.

Throughout my high school years and summers, I would travel with my friends to churches, schools, outside parks, driveways, and, in some cases, to people's private basketball courts to play the sport. Even when I had no one to accompany me, I would find a basket, visualize playing against a theoretical Michael Jordan, forming hypothetical situations to improve my shots. I was particularly determined to boost my vertical jump because even though I was only 6 feet and 1 inch tall, deep down, I knew I was capable of flight to slam dunk that dang ball!

Even before my sophomore year came to an end, I had begun to soar off of one foot and dunk with some power. I found it more exhilarating than ever, so it was no wonder that I wouldn't miss a single chance of doing so. I attribute some degree of this accomplishment of flight to a friend who gave me specially made shoes that strengthen my muscles and increase my ability to jump higher. During the same year, I was on track to be on varsity at a 5A high school as a sophomore, among some exquisite talent by proving myself in stats. However, the hope was short-lived because I sustained an injury during the weeks of tryouts that set me back. By the time I recovered and was approved to resume playing, the stats were done and dusted, and the teams had been established. I considered it bad luck; however, the setback couldn't downplay my passion for the sport. But it taught me a lesson: it wasn't just my skill that helped me make the varsity team so early; it was also having a teammate who was the team captain. At the end of the day, this guy was a true athlete, but even more, he was a real leader on and off the court and an amazing basketball athlete.

I strongly believe that those high school years were a blessing in terms of growing and building our skills. We possessed more talent than anyone else I could remember at that point. Some of my friends went on to play in college, others in leagues overseas, and some even made it to the NBA. Since we all were playing at a high level for our age, and the talent in our circle made us much better players, I can safely say that every one of us could have easily advanced to at least college basketball.

Oftentimes, we used to play against this one giant and athletic NBA-bound hooper, not knowing that he would go to play and win an NBA championship just several years from being drafted right out of high school. Even during those years, he was an inspiration for all of us to play harder. Regardless of the circumstances, he, as well as the mass amount of talent in our town, would drive everyone to become better players and adopt the never give up mantra. Years later, I would watch some of his NBA games and imagine how it would feel to play against the talent he was playing with regard to how well we played against him in his high school years. We definitely would have been hungry and pumped up, but eventually, we would have ended up getting served, to say the least.

Nearly every time I see him in his sportscasting role on television, I can't help recalling the elite NBA workout knowledge he shared about interval training when he returned from his first training camp. He looked like Shaq when he left but transformed into a young, thin Shaq upon return. Those tips formed the foundation for me to fine-tune some things and make the decision to try out for the Navy Seals. I can't thank him enough for his solid workout guidance that enabled me to get in shape and build resilience for the toughest challenges that await me in the future.

Moreover, it's not just about an ideal; basketball is a fast-paced and dynamic sport. Like other organized team sports, it lets you embrace the power of teamwork. It lets you understand that in order to win, you must be truly aware of your team members. If you think about it, it's a critical lesson for any young individual, no matter what their goals are. At different points in time, youngsters choose their teams, which, in turn, paves the way for their selection. Each player has strengths and weaknesses, and everyone should operate knowing those details like a finely tuned Rolex with perfect timing.

Another huge lesson that I got from playing basketball was that the respect you earn by excelling in a sport and winning games and competitions goes way beyond the boundary of the court. I had worked incredibly hard to become ambidextrous, improve my coordination, and defy the laws of gravity to be able to slam dunk a basketball. Even though I knew I would never be able to make it to the NBA, I was giving the sport everything I had. Why? Because it challenged me and drove me to strive as much as I could. It became my passion, and I loved the fact that the harder I worked, the better I performed, which ultimately earned me greater respect on and off the court. In fact, the reputation I built in my never-ending journey to mastering the game stayed with me for decades to come. This was a great lesson I learned as a young man early on in life: Take the time to practice something, master it, earn respect, and see how you prosper. Nonetheless, I loved playing basketball more than anything else at the time, so even if I didn't get those privileges of counting on a career with basketball, putting in those efforts was highly worthwhile.

What I consider to be my favorite basketball achievement was my ability to fly and slam dunk that dang ball in different forms, including windmills, backward, forward, ally-oops, and, at times, over and above some giant players.

Rolling back to a good basketball memory, there was this one time, a game I played back in my high school days at a recreation center. To everyone's surprise and awe, I managed to dunk on a 6'8 guy whom we played in the tournament. He clearly wasn't happy about it and even tried to fight with me, especially because his friends started making fun of him and "clowning" him.

To maintain the peace and be the person I am, I gave the tall guy an opportunity to dunk on me in an off-game setting to "settle" things. As he went up, I noticed his hand coming down on me, and luckily, I threw the ball directly to the ground along with him. He held on to the ball, and no foul was given. Taking a few steps back, I noticed the breakout of more chaos as his friends began clowning him again. This was when this unexpected thing happened: He got up and walked around in an angry state for a few seconds, perhaps to regain his composure, before walking back to me and shaking hands. He accepted what had just happened, and I earned his respect. My buddy Tommy and I are unlikely ever to forget this.

At that point, I experienced a fundamental truth for survival, a truth I later heard from Damon West, a local Southeast, Texas author and national motivational speaker:

"You don't always have to win your fights, but you have to fight all of your fights."

I found that statement to be profoundly true. Even though I always felt I inherently understood this principle, I didn't really think about it until it became relevant to me, which he explained from his own perspective. You either win, or you learn. When you win, small victories pave the way for bigger ones, while the small lessons you learn from failures let you avoid the harder ones that life hurls your way when you least expect them. Like the advice I got from the local Texas Legend Tilman Fertitta's book *Shut Up and Listen*. I read the book before having the chance to listen to him live at the Golden Nugget and attend a book signing. His advice was so simple yet so profound that it resonated with me hard:

"There is a paddle coming for everybody's ass, and you have no idea when it's coming, and you have no idea where it's coming from."

I mean, you hear that, realize it's true, and immediately want to learn how to mitigate the impact of these paddles. So, when the paddle shows up, ensure you have done all you can to be best prepared to take on less damage. But still, putting things together so far, you must fight all of your fights, win or learn, and watch out for paddles if you want to be victorious or successful.

These golden words proved extremely helpful as I prepared for the next stages of my life.

Back in those days, the normal career path for our millennial generation looked like Pre-k, Kindergarten, elementary school, middle school, and high school, after which graduates would start working, attend college, or pursue both. A small number of graduates opt to join the military, from where they venture into the unknown.

I chose to enroll in college and was fortunate enough to find work with a very successful couple that operated multiple businesses that I had known for the majority of my life. Entrepreneurs are inspirational personalities, and this couple was no different. Not only were they highly self-motivated, but they also had an innovative approach to everything. Their competitive spirit was unparalleled, and no matter what, they would never let anything debilitate their strong sense of ethics and integrity. I would envy their bold leadership qualities and willingness to take risks, and unlike many arrogant businessmen of the time, they clearly understood the value of developing and maintaining a strong peer network.

Well aware of their capabilities, I would turn to the couple for mentorship. From questions related to faith to study-related options and decisions, I often sought their advice. They would provide me with very thoughtful ideas and solutions.

During those days, I was faced with a daunting feeling, and I decided to share it with them. I told them how I was dissatisfied working and attending college and was determined to achieve something bigger in life. I elaborated on how my life seemed monotonous and boring, and I wanted to make it more meaningful.

I even shared that by joining the World's Greatest Navy, I could make the difference I am looking to make. Since my nation had recently been attacked and was already at war, it was a perfect time to spark my patriotic self and safeguard my family, friends, and country. I was keen to protect American families and defend the homeland with whatever skills I had and whatever skills I would gain.

The two mentors suggested that when making a pivotal choice in life, it's best to pray about it first. I took their advice, and in what seemed like no time but was actually several months, I would be sworn in to support and defend the United States Constitution by serving my role in the Navy. I made the biggest decision in my life, signing up for the unknown in the name of democracy and freedom for a purpose much greater than myself.

My goal was to become a Navy Seal, but ironically, I was convinced to sign up for the Intelligence Community by a Navy SEAL who had suffered damage in the line of duty and was serving temporary duty in Chicago at the boot camp. His advice was to learn all that intel has to offer before you become an operator because then you will have more to offer. Honestly speaking, I had absolutely no idea what I was getting myself into, yet the job description appealed to me. It wasn't an impulsive decision; I took the time to consult experts in the field and was still enticed by what I was told. The decision made more sense at the time because it was 2005, the post-9/11 environment. The US intelligence was in dire need of talented minds and physically capable bodies. Hence, I signed my name in the contract to be an Intelligence Specialist with the option to try out for the SEALS and got sworn in.

Chapter 2: The Navy

"I have not yet begun to fight!"

If you have served in the Navy, you are well aware of the historic naval hero John Paul Jones, who, in the midst of a battle, took on great damage and, instead of surrendering, uttered those heroic words. For me, I joined the Navy to fight and defend my Constitution and my country, and for those who are not able to defend themselves. At this stage, the last thought I would ever have was that one day, I would be fighting for my own freedom against members of my own team. Not just the Navy but the entire weight of the Armed Forces. But, back to boot camp for now.

Granted, the conditions at any boot camp are never easy. The day I got enlisted, training was at the top of my mind. I knew that I would be spending most of my initial months undergoing continuous training and would get opportunities to learn skills. I knew I was going to a harsh, solemn environment. Thus, September 2005 was when I and my life became much more serious.

Depending on the service branch, the 6 to 13 weeks of your time at the boot camp is extremely intense and rigorous. If you possess the courage to succeed, the training will transform you into a fully capable service member. You tend to be highly motivated and determined to deliver your best and learn new skills, including patience. You walk out as a mature and more disciplined individual, no matter how well-disciplined you already were.

That being said, a lot happened between that first and the last day. Given the demanding nature of the training, what lasted just a few weeks felt like years. During this time, drill instructors guided us on how to take care of ourselves and others, work as a team, and accomplish success together. They were responsible for ensuring that the recruits were fully prepared to face challenges, including the rigors of the battlefield and the dangers of life at sea. We were given the necessary tools to perform our tasks with confidence, courage, and efficacy to succeed in the face of adversity, and while not facing adversity, we also kept things maintained, clean, and organized. Aside from the seriousness of the mission, sailors will always laugh if someone brings up jokes about several skills that they program us to do better than 99 percent of society, such as ironing, folding clothes, shining boots, sewing, mopping, and shining brass. But yes, indeed, there were some key takeaways from the training, which included first aid, marksmanship, water survival skills, and other tactics.

The first few days were a blur when we were exposed to incessant loud yelling that started from our bus ride in and continued for about three days straight until we progressed. In the following days, we were expected to stand or sit in line while they passed us through injection stations and other formalities to process us. Throughout this time, they made sure we stayed awake. From time to time, someone in uniform would be by our side to ensure that we didn't fall asleep. Yes, some trainees would pass out. To this day, I still have no recollection of what or how many shots we received, but there were a lot. I mostly just remember a bunch of bald slapheads looking about as tired as they probably could.

To embark on the training, I and other recruits were supposed to fly out of Houston, but unfortunately, a category 5 hurricane was on its way to the city. Since people were being evacuated and were in a state of panic in trying to flee the hurricane, the traffic was chaotic during the day. Our cab driver from our hotel to the airport was subject to urgency. Upon entering the mostly empty airport, we were given a heads up that it was possible that the plane would not take off that day, in which case we wouldn't be able to depart on time and would have to wait for weeks or even months to leave for boot camp. Upon hearing this, I told myself, "Well, if this plane doesn't take off today, it must be a signal from up above, and I will be retracting my enlistment promise and going home."

As fate would have it, ours was the last flight approved by the airport and the government that day to fly because it was serving for military purposes. Hence, we rolled down the runway through the rain, pressed forward, gained elevation, and were on our way to the Navy Boot Camp in Chicago, Illinois, with a Category 5 hurricane on our tail.

The hurricane situation made the boot camp transition a little tougher for us, more so than for others, who could have, at some point in time, called home and spoken to family and friends. In our case, however, no communication could be established because our hometowns had been destroyed. As we passed by televisions every so often while attending to administrative matters some days at boot camp, we would capture glimpses of news showing the devastation from the storm. For weeks, all sorts of thoughts about our families kept haunting us, and it wasn't until the end of the boot camp that we managed to get ahold of our families. For many of us, this was the longest we had been away from our families; imagine not being able to make calls to know whether your loved ones were okay, whom you'd left in a devastated area that was to take years to recover.

Even when I was able to make home visits afterward, I witnessed mountains of debris from torn-down homes and knocked-over trees, piles of which persisted for years following Category 5 Hurricane Rita. For your information, hurricane Rita was not only the most intense tropical cyclone on record in the Gulf of Mexico but also the fourth most intense Atlantic hurricane ever recorded. Characterized by wind gusts of up to 180 mph, the catastrophe led to a staggering $18.5 billion in damage in 2005. Every time our sights caught these facts and figures in the news while moving around the boot camp, we would cringe, for we were totally disconnected from our homes.

As part of their trend to break us down, they would shave our heads at some point so that we all appeared the same. This was when all the paperwork was being done and uniforms were being issued. At the time of the first military issue of uniforms, we mailed all our personal belongings back to our homes. This symbolized and reinforced the change in us, emphasizing the death of the old and the birth of the new.

Thankfully, I realized in a timely manner that boot camp was mostly a mind game designed to take the civilian out of you and instill in you a top-notch military service member. I kept telling myself that thousands of young men and women had survived it before me, so there was no reason why I couldn't do it. There were many people around in our division that I personally witnessed people just lose from time to time, but for me, even the hard days weren't that hard compared to what was to come. In a Forrest Gump-like turn of events, I personally made a best friend from Alabama, with whom I would later deploy, room, and become lifetime friends. When times were tough, we would usually work out or trash talk about Texas and Alabama football. I still, to this day, will never forget the non-stop stories, facts, and statistics of the legendary football coach Paul Bear Bryant, Nick Saban, and the University of Alabama's 12, now 18 titles at the time. I'm sure when he reads, he will inevitably yell to himself or aloud, "Roll Tide," for no apparent reason.

To survive the boot camp while steering clear of trouble, I also set up some rules for myself. First, I decided to maintain a good attitude. I would tell myself that everyone gets chewed out in the boot camp, even when they performed well, and that things wouldn't be this way after I graduate from the training. Second, I promised myself never to make excuses. I knew that explanations were seen as excuses unless you were asked to explain yourself. Being from

Texas, saying "Yes, sir," was natural and helpful in avoiding any nonsense. Third, I planned to avoid being inventive and do exactly what I was told to do, including when and how they needed to be done. Finally, I also made it a habit to be where I was supposed to be fifteen minutes early because being 'on time' in the boot camp meant you were late.

It wouldn't be wrong to say that if it weren't for these golden rules that I set for myself, I wouldn't have survived the boot camp. They proved to be a gem through all the ups and downs of the period, letting me endure everything with a smile, no matter how much things sucked. In those "sucky" times, I learned to embrace them. I picked up that little tool from someone who was telling a story of their hard times and called it "embracing the suck," which just made sense to me and stuck.

A lot happened during my Navy boot camp training, and there are plenty of stories to tell revolving around different aspects of the boot camp and many other stories past boot camp when the time is right. Those stories will be saved for later book discussions. If you are interested, let me give you a feel of how the grueling period concluded. Toward the end of the boot camp, we were exposed to a simulated wartime environment called battle stations. In this setting, you and your division are challenged to apply all the knowledge acquired and the leadership skills developed through the 8-week boot camp's team-building process.

This marks an exciting yet emotional time for the trainees because, on the one hand, it exhibits a critical moment when you win the battle, while on the other, you transition from a Navy Recruit to a Navy Sailor. This happened right after the end of the simulation events when everyone was overly exhausted, trying their best to stay awake and, in some cases, crying. Some of the tears stemmed from joy, while others erupted for reasons known only to God.

We stood there confused, getting yelled at and praised at the same time, trying to guess what comes next in our lives. Then began the ceremony of compelling speeches, though they communicated to us about what it was that we had accomplished and earned. We were issued what's referred to as 'ball caps' in the Navy jargon, so we were able to switch our 'Recruit' ball caps to 'Navy' ball caps. After we were congratulated, we went off to have the first breakfast that we were able to make a choice about. No doubt it was well deserved. This is when we felt some relief, realizing that we had advanced to a phase of the Navy where we could expect a bit of normalcy.

As we stuffed our faces with food during that breakfast, we laughed and cried, reflecting on the specific instances of battling through the day and night until it came to an end. We soon marched our graduating class, along with many others, across the hangar in Chicago, saluting the Master Chief Petty Officer of The Navy (MCPON) as we were graduating and sent off to our first training commands. My first command was the Navy & Marine Corps Intelligence Training Center, which would be much longer than the several months in Chicago, but hey, I was moving on with life and this great opportunity at the Beach. A beach that would change my life forever with memories of service, good friends, bright minds, clean sand, and good beer. A beach that would also lead me to our entire boot camp top graduate, where she and I became good friends and dated for a time later in the future.

Chapter 3: The UCI

"The worst form of injustice is pretended justice."

The aforementioned quote from an ancient Greek philosopher, Plato, couldn't be more accurate in portraying what I've faced in my life. To be honest, it has been a bitter pill to swallow and led me to lose most trust in the country's judicial system. I had been a highly accomplished student and performer all my life who would excel in just about anything I decided to pursue. I also remained a diligent service member in the US military and always sought to push beyond limits to serve my country. But all of a sudden, something happened, and my career fell to pieces.

With a heavy heart, I am here, ready to narrate how the worst exercise of Unlawful Command Influence (UCI) in the history of the US military occurred and was used to target myself and others. But before I get into that, let me explain the concept of UCI.

Unlawful Command Influence (UCI) usually occurs in two forms: actual unlawful command influence and apparent unlawful command influence. An example is when a military commander leverages their authority to intervene, in an unfair manner, with a service member's court-martial. They influence the lower commander's judgment to either make certain recommendations on charges or prefer charges against the service member. It can be carried out by a commander at any level. According to appellate courts, UCI is the mortal enemy of the military justice system.

UCI is a breach of Article 37 of the Uniform Code of Military Justice (UCMJ), according to which no authority convening a general, special, or summary court-martial, nor any other commanding officer can admonish, censure, or reprimand the court of any member, counsel, or military judge, with respect to the sentence or findings adjudged by the court. It also declares that no person may attempt to force or by any unauthorized means affect the action of any military tribunal or court-martial.[1]

Let me also shed some light on the background of this terrible instance of UCI. In 2012, the government bodies under Obama's administration were subject to numerous changes. I can assume that since he had won his re-election and did not have to truly stand by a single word he campaigned for, he couldn't lose his job, and he was going to be gone in several years. I do not want to criticize him directly, but his leadership style did well and not so well, depending on the topic, agenda, or mission. This included the revered Title IX policies and guidance that was ultimately found to be nothing more than a compilation of unofficially sanctioned ideas from the Department of Education that went on to destroy the college life of so many young Americans.

Unfortunately, this unlawful, misleading guidance eventually made its way into the military because whosoever possessed the power of the purse in politics could do

---

[1] https://openscholarship.wustl.edu/cgi/viewcontent.cgi?article=6226&context=law_lawreview

anything they wanted to. This was when the Senate, House, and Presidency were dominated by a single party. In a situation like this, it's common for people to do whatever they want, and if a decision proves unpopular at some point in the future, they would simply ask for forgiveness. In no time, UCI started surfacing in the military. In the very beginning, I even noticed UCI happening in one of my training sessions and had no way of knowing how to respond. So, I decided the best course of action was to stay silent. I had no idea that many years later, I would become a victim of this UCI plague. Lesson learned here: staying silent leads to more problems. Follow your gut and make noise if things don't seem right.

The level at which the UCI was exercised against the Armed Forces, and myself was unlike anything the world had ever seen. Literally. Only after a while did I realize how many people and leadership from all branches of service were involved. UCI, in my case, was an environment-shaping tool apparently invented by the administration to include the President, governmental departments, and all of the senior leadership in the government. The media played a critical role in assisting the agenda. An agenda that worked like a computer operating system executing all the elements of shaping military environments, such as propaganda, the use of technology, IO, media exploits, the mainstream media, and most importantly, the use of the human element: people.

So, what exactly was the agenda? To explain this, I'll need to go right to the root of it.

It all seems to have started when Michell Obama assigned April as a Sexual Assault Awareness month in 2010. Since around 108,121 veterans screened positive for military sexual trauma in 2010 alone, the assigning was shown to be based on a virtuous cause but was actually part of a much larger and damaging agenda in the history of the military. This started becoming obvious when, in May 2013, President Obama conducted UCI by publicly identifying the military as a target for rooting out whoever engages in sexual assault or is even accused of, while also directing the then Secretary Chuck Hagel to "exponentially go after it." This would be one year after the time that the young lady and myself had hung out together. Essentially, he had just let loose the cavalry on me and people like me.

What acted as one of the strongest forces in this so-called 'sexual assault campaign' was the release of the film 'The Invisible War.' This 2012 American documentary film featured interviews of veterans from various branches of the US Armed Forces who shared their stories of sexual assaults. Some of the themes it revolved around included the absence of adequate physical and emotional care of survivors, lack of recourse to an impartial justice system, forced expulsion of survivors from service, reprisals against survivors instead of against perpetrators, and continued advancement of perpetrators' careers.

During this time, the media played a crucial role in creating hype about the sexual assault campaign. The government has the power of the purse over public education, so they went after colleges using the Department of Education (DOE) with unsanctioned rules that acted with the weight of law in the Title IX realm. This is why schools were having a similar reaction to that of what we were experiencing. Flipping lives upside down through unsanctioned "Dear colleague" guidance that was proven to have never supposed to have held the weight of rule or law. The pain, suffering, and damages, without a real way to conduct personal damage control, led to suicides stemming just from accusations; some were even cleared and found not guilty after it was too late. Then came the lawsuits, which were a big deal on the education front, but that did not do much for service members; as of the time, one could not launch a lawsuit at the military with any expectation of having a positive impact; hence, no one did. But again, the media was playing the game of government for the "home team," if you will. Even the slightest mentions of potential sexual assault convictions against service members were amplified and portrayed in outrageously exaggerated versions, regardless of whether the accusations against them were true or not. On the one hand, the media's influence exerted a silent demand on administrators to take action against the accused, while on the other, it created an environment of urgency for sensitive cases.

Everyone agrees that sexual assault is bad and the perceived problem in the military was also adequate, but how exactly it was dealt with paved the way for mass prejudice and massive injustice.

Among the call to action put forth by the producer of 'The Invisible War' to Secretary of Defense Leon Panetta was to move the decision to investigate and prosecute a sexual assault claim outside the victim's chain of command. As for my case, it was handled by civilian authorities outside my chain of command, and their decision-making appears to have been unaffected by the UCI, but the military is a federal entity that can later act on what's called a right of first refusal by the state; the state dropped the investigation and cleared me indefinitely. The right of first refusal allowed the military to continue to pursue me against what evidence revealed suggested my innocence. Even the detective lamented in his dismissal of the investigation for lack of evidence and wrote on the official documentation, dropping any charges from the State and noting that the Navy has an "invested interest" in this case. Mind you, I was at an Army base and under their jurisdiction while being investigated by a seasoned and well-respected local law enforcement agent and the Army CID. This invested interest implies he was aware of the mishandling and the environment of the time. It makes sense why training conducted by the influential Judge Advocate Lieutenant Colonel Palmer, who is a critical node regarding the greater problem, included the following key comments regarding teaching Judge Advocates how to do their jobs serving justice:

- "Defendants are scumbags."

- "The defendant is guilty. We wouldn't be at this stage if he wasn't guilty."

- "As trial counsel, it is your job to prove the defendant is guilty with the fullest veracity. Don't hold back. Once convicted, we need to crush these Marines and get them out."

- "Once the convening authority decides to proceed with the charges, you must have a willing suspension of disbelief of the victims."

In a UCI environment like this, it was no wonder that each decision point in the flow of my case acted like a prescription from statements derived from UCI events. If you check my charge sheet, it's clear how the idea to "put charges on paper even if unprovable" was implemented. Among all the unprovable charges added to my charge sheet, the last one was the most unprovable. It stated, "To wit that I had to have known that the Lance Corporal was unable to consent." In other words, in my own mind, I should have known she was unable to consent to anything. Yes, the prosecutor proposed that in my mind, I was supposed to have the foresight to know that this person could not consent, although she functioned, walked, talked, and flirted like a champion. But back to the greater problem.

Since the convening authorities were forced by the hand leadership above them rather than making the recommendations based on the merits of the case, any charges that are made would inevitably advance to court martial. Based on the second comment stated above, they were established as 'guilty' just because they had to be.

The same influential JAG, Palmer, is also reported to have implicitly expressed that jury members are stupid, knuckle-dragging morons that need to have the drool wiped away from their mouths and that he doesn't hate them but despises them. This was merely a ploy to keep fairness out of the results by swaying those accused to have a court-martial by a judge alone and not use their given right to a trial by jury.

So, how did I become a victim of UCI?

Well, in November 2012, a woman I had been casually dating, Lance Corporal H., invited me to meet her at a bar off-base but then asked me to pick her up on base instead. Although it had only been a couple of weeks since I first met her, both of us got interested in each other, texting and talking periodically. Even though it was quite late, I accepted her invitation. Not only was Lance Corporal H. happy to see me, but we also flirted throughout the meetup. On one occasion, we joked about her not wearing any panties, and on the dance floor, she even made a gesture that was representative of her giving me a "BJ." Hence, it was pretty clear where all this might be heading, even though I truly had no intention of taking it any further than a meet-up and hang-out. People who know me know that during this time of my life, I loved to be out among people and meet new people, hear their stories, and, of course, flirt and dance.

While Lance Corporal H. was drinking, she wasn't drunk. The entire evening, she had a total of three drinks, namely two drinks of pineapple juice and coconut rum mixed with one shot of Goldschlager. There's no evidence that she consumed any other type of intoxicant that night. This was also later validated by the drug screening she had done the next day at her pre-scheduled medical appointment that was ordered because she made a statement to medical that she was not feeling well prior to that morning.

After spending a few hours at the club, we mutually decided to go to my apartment, so Lance Corporal H. walked outside the bar with me in a well-balanced manner. I had a Jeep Wrangler, so its seat was fairly elevated. Yet, she managed to climb in on her own many times as she spoke to her friend, who, to me, felt more like a handler. However, this indicated that she was in her right state of mind and wasn't overly intoxicated. In fact, she climbed out to talk to a friend and then climbed back in without requiring any assistance.

Next, Lance Corporal H. expressed that they wanted to accompany me to my apartment, and while on the way, we kept on flirting with each other. Upon arriving at my apartment, she jumped out of my jeep and walked up the three flights of stairs to my apartment. While rising up the stairs, she walked and talked, normally facing no problems in tackling the three flights of stairs. Once we were inside the apartment, we kissed, caressed, and groped each other - an attempt at sex followed. We also had an encounter a second time when we woke up in the morning when she sat down next to me in a towel and let it down.

I looked at her and said, "Well, somebody is motivated this morning. Do you want me to get a condom?"

She simply replied with a yes, nodding her head. So even though I was hesitant because of the time that the cab driver would arrive, I had a female naked next to me asking me to put a condom on. This younger version of me fell right into it, letting her foreplay get me in the mood and get the condom on. After I got the condom on, my soldier, so to speak, couldn't stand attention because it was too tight and cutting off my circulation, which happened during our last attempt earlier in the morning. So, she continued with foreplay as I tried to become appropriate. The farthest that event went was us rubbing the condom with my flaccid penis in it, repeatedly trying to get to the sex part, I suppose. However, it was not happening, and I gave up. The condom wasn't made for my size, and therefore, I knew it wasn't going to happen. I explained to her it wasn't her fault and why I couldn't get it off. I did, against good sense, ask if she wanted me to try without the condom; however, her reply was, "No, let's stop. I am sore down there anyhow." Sometime shortly after, when the cab driver called me for the pickup, I walked out to the door and asked her to please give the passenger a minute as time had slipped away. This was while she was getting dressed. Following her getting dressed, the last time we spoke in person was when she was leaving to go to the cab. Before she opened the door and walked out in a sort of odd manner, she stopped fast on me and asked when I was leaving town and if our fling would continue any longer. I was leaving in a few days, which she knew, so I just looked at her from the sofa, and all I could think to say was, "Are you being serious right now?" To me, it just seemed strange because we had already implied our grounds before any of our engagements. When I first met her, she was telling me about her night out of being promiscuous and sleeping with someone the night before that she would never talk to again. She knew I was leaving, and we both expressed short-term interest. It came out of nowhere and was rushed in a very unnatural manner as she was hustling trying to get to the cab, which had been waiting for an extended amount of time from the initial phone call. I couldn't put my finger on it at the time, but that brief interaction just had a bad vibe to it. We went from revisiting sex to having a short and speedy conversation on a topic that usually demands at least more than a mere few seconds. In fact, I would go as far as to say that not in any way, shape or form a "hey, I am in a hurry. Let me throw a topic that takes time, maturity, and reasoning into a 5-second conversation." That was a conversation to have at a later time. She had my number and could have easily called or texted to talk about the details of the arrangements. So when she left that morning, I had absolutely no idea what truly happened other than what was stated at the court martial. To be candid, honestly, if she ever felt like she had been wronged, that wasn't ever explicitly concluded either. Because our time together was "normal" despite the last few seconds before she left, I have no idea how the accusation truly became an accusation, and I have no idea what her true motive was. In her initial victim impact letter, she plainly states that "she felt like she had been dragged along by the military." In contrast, in addition to her statements at court-martial, it frankly provides reasonable evidence that she never intended to make an accusation against me. However, the military forced their agenda, in my opinion.

Sometime later, and seemingly as if out of nowhere, I got a phone call from a civilian investigator, asking questions that I frankly didn't know how to answer, as I didn't know if it was legitimate, someone messing with me, or a scorned lover because in my world it could have all been possible. Ultimately, while I was feeling out about this person's intentions, I finally asked what the true purpose of the call was. The answer was, of course, that there was an accusation of sexual assault based on the theory that she "was incapable of consenting to the sexual act due to her impairment by an intoxicant." This has always been a mystery to me because not only was I courteous in calling and paying for her a taxi to get her to her scheduled doctor appointment on time, but even during court-martial, she directly stated that the text messages between her and her immediate supervisor for whatever reason were not ever supposed to be handled in any manner outside of their conversation, while also stating that she never asked anyone to accuse me of anything. It even reached the point where my defense attorneys simply asked, "Then why are we here?" because she claimed not to know why. Her answer was, "I don't know." This was more than telling me that whoever was out for me was using the Unlawful Command Influence (UCI) to get me to a predetermined outcome of guilt, no matter what was presented in court. To this day, I have absolutely no idea what those text messages contain. This also means that there is no initial complaint. If you were to look into the entire case file, you would be left with one single question: where did the complaint come from?

Until this time, not even a single complaint had been filed against me through my tenure in the military. This thought kept popping up in my mind during the two years of investigation that I had not previously known was going on and while waiting to know whether I would face a trial by Court Martial. Since the very start, I wasn't bothered or worried about the accusation because, most importantly, the claims were baseless, and secondly, I knew I was innocent. As usual, I continued my training to prepare for deployments and had to undergo surgery after sustaining some training injuries. Needless to say, this was a rough time in my career.

During this period, my service date as per the contract came to an end, and for personal reasons, I decided to transfer my efforts out of the Navy and seek commissioning in the Coast Guard, which was also closer to my home. However, things didn't go as planned because the military chain of authorities and administration office extended my contract several times until the decision about my prosecution was made. This was until someone finally was brazen enough to persecute me, for they had the mortal enemy of military justice by their side, that is, unlawful command influence.

Quite ridiculously, the trial advanced to a court-martial situation, and in her testimony, she denied remembering everything from walking out of the bar to walking up the three flights of stairs to my apartment. According to her, the last thing she remembered before the sexual encounter was standing in the bar, after which she only remembered waking up with me having sex with her at some point. In other words, the prosecution tried to imply that the sexual engagement wasn't consensual and that I carried her out of the club, put her in my car, carried her up three flights of stairs, and had sex with her when she wasn't even awake or in her senses. To back her claim that she was unconscious the entire time, she made yet another story that upon waking up with me on top of her, I assured her, "Don't worry, I used a condom." However, she could vividly remember so many other intermittent details, including what exact shirt I was wearing, yet again, only strategically answered questions that would give the prosecution some hope of justifying even holding a court martial at all. Everything that mattered, the answer was "I don't know."

During that night, she texted and talked with friends at various points in time, which couldn't have been possible if she hadn't been able to function. Therefore, even though they were prosecuting an innocent man, and all of the details didn't make sense, given the highly uncertain and volatile environment, my counsel chose to exercise my constitutional right to remain silent. I knew and could see UCI happening but couldn't do anything about it, quite similar to how I couldn't do anything when I first noticed UCI developing after learning about psychological, information, propaganda, and environment-shaping operations.

Think about it thus far. Ask yourself, how can someone even attempt to claim being impaired by an intoxicant when they climbed onto my Jeep Wrangler twice on their own and walked up the three flights of stairs to my apartment? All she had was three drinks over several hours of time, which could not and did not make Lance Corporal H. incapable of consenting. She was fully awake and was just as active in our attempt at sexual engagement as me.

What's more shocking and important here is that the military judge took Lance Corporal H.'s words verbatim as if they were the gospel itself and convicted me of sexual assault. Stating that Lance Corporal H. was incapable of consenting to the sexual act due to her impairment by an intoxicant, the military judge solely relied on her false testimony and sealed my fate. What the judge deemed as the "key in establishing" that Lance Corporal H. was not awake due to being intoxicated was her claim of me assuring her that I used a condom. I never said anything like that, and I was stunned when the military judge blindly took her words, even though she was the only person with an abundance of inconsistencies in their statements.

Therefore, Lance Corporal H. either lied about not remembering the details or experienced a memory blackout.

Her condom-related lie indicates everything she said about not remembering was also a lie. And even if she had a memory blackout, it doesn't necessarily mean she could not consent to sex. She was kissing me, was eager to have sex with me, and was a consensual and active participant. The most important element of all of this regarding her testimony, which was taken as fact even though she was aware of the trail of inconsistent statements, was this: if she could not consent, then neither could I. However, the law of consent is clear, and when referred to, it will explain that we both were well within the range of consent and not even close to being unable to consent. Without this consideration by the judge in a matter of minutes, I was stripped of everything a service member or person can own and hold dearly after a decade of hard work and quality service to my country.

The laws of consent are fairly clear, with more than enough case law from expert witnesses regarding the psychological aspects of consent. So again, the judge decided that she couldn't consent, which implied I could, even though it was never brought to question, and the only person inconsistent with any incentive to lie was her. So we could both drive legally. However, we could not mutually engage in our activity that evening according to our judge, but not to actual law. However, I am the one who has been paying the price ever since. A heavy price. I will say this about our decision to not take the stand: pleading the 5th didn't save me this decade of pain so far. However, it does allow anyone to review the case and plainly see exactly what the government did because it was a transcript of only them and their witnesses.

Even though the accuser's testimonies and evidence were full of inconsistencies, the military judge considered the accuser credible. After comparing multiple statements that should have read the same information to everyone, everyone had a different variant of her story than what was given directly from her own mouth every single time. Even a rather large group of JAG trainees who sat in the back found me innocent at that time. That was not a big deal to the judge, apparently, but what was important was that he stated that the past tense of the word 'used' in the statement 'Don't worry, I used a condom' proves that I knew that the plaintiff was unable to consent. Even if I had made that statement, it didn't establish that sexual assault had been committed because the statement, by no means, proves the accuser's inability to consent, nor even near the burden necessary to convict. Ultimately, those words mean someone used a condom. It's nothing new. I can Imagine we've all seen on television, heard of, or participated in a heat-of-the-moment fast track to sex and either before, during, or after question the use of a condom once hormones have calmed down.

The standard to prove the plaintiff's inability to consent should have been to show that the plaintiff had consumed enough alcohol to not be in her senses at the time of sexual activity or be in a position to agree or disagree with the alleged sexual conduct. In the 3- to 4-hour window, she had only three drinks and demonstrated having many intermittent memories of times before, during, and after the sexual activity. She could vividly describe my clothes, personal Information openly shared with her, and other details; however, she couldn't remember anything "Important."

It turned out the evidence used to judge that I was guilty itself was full of suspicions. The statement attributed to me, 'Don't worry, I used a condom,' greatly evolved over the course of the case. In December 2012, the plaintiff stated in her account with the Army CID that I said, "I have a condom on" during sexual activity, which is more of an answer to a question to a person who is conscious. For some reason, as soon as a Special Victim Advocate (SVA) or personal attorney was assigned to the plaintiff, the account of that statement changed, and where the inconsistent statements began, things started making less sense.

More suspicions could be sensed in the plaintiff's 'I don't know' response to multiple questions. Little did I know that these were all tactics aligned with UCI guidance to set up a conviction to get past the burden shift of court-martial. The game is that once convicted, the burden shifts to the defense, and the bar is set higher, which is quite unfair, especially to an innocent person. Yet, things went exactly as planned, in my opinion. In no time, my case transitioned into appeals, where the shift made justice more and more difficult as the courts were dealing with an overload of cases that I believe they weren't prepared to handle and didn't give cases the reviews they deserved. But again, the case against me shouldn't have gotten as far as it did, and the prosecution should still be responsible for proving beyond a reasonable doubt that this person could not consent. Since there was no evidence to prove or even imply that the sexual activity was consensual, because you can't prove innocence in a case like mine, these malicious tactics that fit the UCI agenda were the only way to go. Also, the plaintiff's own words, "I don't remember saying 'no' or 'stop,'" were clear evidence that everything that happened between her and me was consensual.

There were other explanations for why Lance Corporal H.'s claims were not credible. For example, after waking up that morning and having another romantic encounter with her, while she dressed and got her things together, I called a taxi to take her back to the base. In the taxi driver's testimony, she stated that she picked Lance Corporal H. up from outside my apartment, stemming from a male who called in. This is true, but not according to Lance Corporal H.'s inconsistent statements of first stating that she called a taxi herself, then changing it to not calling herself but just walking out and finding the nearest taxi that just happened to be right there. Anyone who has been to this area knows that taxis don't just sit anywhere outside your place in the morning. Then, once picked up, she had an hour-long conversation on the way to the base and stopped somewhere to buy soda and cigarettes. When asked during her testimony about this trip, Lance Corporal H. said she had no memory of the hour-long conversation with the driver nor about stopping somewhere to buy soda and cigarettes.

Similarly, a few months before the trial, Lance Corporal H. had told the investigators about having dinner with me at Applebee's, but on the day of the trial, she said she couldn't remember the details of the meetup or even whether she was with me at Applebee's. The reason was that this also never happened.

These instances clearly showed that Lance Corporal H. may have been experiencing a memory blackout, which was possible for young social drinkers even when they consume small amounts of alcohol, yet she testified that she was a drinker and had a good tolerance to alcohol. Yet again, a memory blackout about the specific night doesn't mean that the sexual activity wasn't consensual because, in memory blackouts, the part of the brain that records memories could stop functioning, but the decision-making portions remain unharmed and keep functioning as normal.

The military judge failed to take into account or consider the possibility that Lance Corporal H. could be lying or may have been experiencing memory blackouts. He likely did this because she was the only witness, and my defense attorney in a normal court would have successfully impeached the government accuser and the star witness. Not only did the judge blindly take her words about the incident, but they also ignored the fact that had her claims been true, someone inside or outside the bar would have seen me carrying an unconscious woman to my jeep and taken steps to prevent this, or at least question it at minimum. That wouldn't happen, though, because, as I stated, she was walking around quite well. This would also be a tough battle for them because she was mostly the initiator in all things, even to the extent of being pushy about staying with me after I declined to stay in a motel room with her and her friend. The way she left her friend behind to come stay with me normally wouldn't have raised any real red flags because friends do that sort of thing. Now, I question absolutely everything. Even though I never had any real plans and was just being "me," it would appear in hindsight that they had some sort of plan I wasn't aware of, and I didn't find out what it was, nor an altered form of it. All that I do know is that when I declined, I could see the frustration in her friend's gestures, which could also explain her being pushy about convincing me to stay with the two of them and then additionally about coming with me after consulting her friend. Again, none of this would help me because the playbook was set up for unfair and impartial jury pools or a single judge's decision.

The fact that the influential leader, Palmer, hated jury members explains why my fate was given in the hands of a single military judge. This tactic facilitated the task of building up and winning a case from nothing. I was very shocked when the judge never talked about all the UCI-type events and statements that were being made at the time. In fact, they did not even acknowledge the existence of those statements in my case, but they did in several cases during the weeks before, during, and after mine. A high-profile case with a Navy Seal was made an example, while the other high-echelon leaders were also in court at the same time. There was no escaping the UCI, but again, not one mention of it in my case, and no one would bring it up for me, almost as if they were fearful, too. Later, we learned that this was mostly correct because new JAGs and those reaching higher ranks wanted to ensure they did not go against the grain and chose self-preservation over justice.

So again, no one ever considered the fact that, exactly like the accuser, I was also drinking that night. We were both drinking, right? Then, how come only one of us had the right to consent, and the other person's state went unquestioned throughout the course of the trial or case? Based on testimony, both of us drank alcohol and engaged in sexual activity the same night, but somehow, the male participant was deemed guilty of sexual assault, while the female participant could not consent. Just as the military judge on Lance Corporal H.'s account of events alone concluded that she couldn't consent to sex, what stopped them from considering that I had also consumed alcohol and couldn't consent? This begs the question, had I myself been sexually assaulted? If I had been, evidently, nobody cared enough to even ask now that I know the law regarding this topic very well.

In this case, either we both should be guilty of sexual assault, or both should be victims. At any point in the trial, I never expressed that I consented, and based on the rules they were following, I was not even in a state where I could consent even though the American Psychological Association (APA), forensic psychologists, Civilian, and Military law know that we were both able to consent at our level of impairment.

Ignoring all this evidence and possibilities, the military judge concluded that I conducted a sexual assault on Lance Corporal H. when she was incapable of consenting to sex due to impairment from alcohol and to wit that I myself should have known she was unable to consent. This led to my court martial. But think critically here and determine for yourself, how could I be aware of her being able to consent when the entire legal chain of command couldn't even figure that out? You are probably seeing things come together at this point, which I commend you on. If not, there is plenty more to learn about.

Unfortunately, the litigation occurred at a time when the entire sexual assault agenda and the associated unlawful command influence were at their peak. Notably, near the beginning of this new agenda, the military began incentivizing individuals who made accusations of sexual assault. Those who came forward would receive favorable treatment, such as choice orders for their next assignment and financial benefits that would last a lifetime upon discharge.

Yet, to this day, the fact that the handling and results of my case were impacted by the UCI environment that prevailed has never been brought up. Back in those days, I reached out to many counsels, asking them to raise this argument, but not even one would. The fact that my case and those similar to it can't make their way into the courtroom today is proof that my court-martial was an outcome of UCI and that I was and still am an innocent United States Sailor. In fact, I spoke with several lead prosecutors in Washington, D.C., where high-ranking individuals work while I was doing my diligence, and it was unbelievably unanimous in their professional opinions that my case would not make it to a court martial. But why? What changed? In 2022, I even spoke to the attorney who represented me at trial as he had climbed the ranks and was well seasoned at this point and may have more information, and what he said explained it all. He simply told me, "I do believe the surrounding circumstances of the time played a major part in the outcome" of my case and then went on to say, "I fully believe that the politics of the time had a major impact on this case and many others at the time."

Hence, facing injustice isn't easy, especially if you've worked hard all your life to reach goals and try to have a positive impact in this world. I had been nearly commissioned twice, received intel work-related accolades, would say I was favored to an extent solely based on performance, and even received a Letter of accommodation from a senior intelligence officer just weeks before I received a charge sheet. It's no wonder that the case took a toll on my emotions, stirring painful feelings like frustration and sadness, but also a drive to never stop until I got to the bottom of how this happened and figured out who or what was responsible. Why shouldn't I channel my anger for good when it wasn't my fault? Channeling anger for the wrong reasons only makes things worse, so in the beginning, I would often find myself in repeated states of shock and engaged in orienting myself in such a way that could assist in discerning what was most important, such as who actually accused me, but also figuring out a way to seek justice against every individual who played a role in the implementation of this worse UCI in US military history. Any advances on our front would plant the seeds of hope of saving veterans and members of the armed forces from such horrific times that I cannot truly put into words how difficult they truly were. Call it a miscarriage of justice, or whatever you may, but as it has been said, the guilty should go free rather than have one innocent person spend one day in prison. As someone who has experienced this from the inside out, I agree wholeheartedly with this idea. It does make me wonder how those leaders who stand by this principle could have such knowledge. Did they philosophically come to that conclusion, or were they of the few who knew from experience the effects this can have on a person? Whatever the reason, it's absolutely true. What's bothersome about having to take a deep dive into justice is that people who have no real experience of what the accusation, punishment, or collateral damages in life after are truly like. Unfortunately, these types of judgments occur every day. Just look at the courts now and how they have weaponized the system for political purposes against opposing parties. If they can do that to the elite, it doesn't take a rocket scientist to imagine how corrupt they can be.

A paradigm shift in my thinking came long after the initial and repeated instances of negative neurological responses of shock and the terrible mind games that wouldn't seem to stop. But, at some point, I realized grumbling about injustice doesn't improve the situation, nor does thinking of those who came against me as hostile. I learned to focus more objectively while learning how to channel my fears and anxieties for good to effectively address the things that need fixing, and I started leaning harder on my faith in God. There's this famous quote from a renowned artist, Mary Engelbreit:

"If you don't like something, change it. If you can't change it, change the way you think about it."

Since I knew I was right, I was not prepared to change the way I thought. Thus, I took up the challenge to change the system and seek justice, not just for myself but for every individual who suffered some form of UCI.

At the same time, I knew that you couldn't bring about a positive change with a negative mindset. To access our personal power, we need to stop seeing ourselves as victims. Possibly, we just need to understand that we are, or might be, and then get back to life. For this reason, I replaced my obsessive thinking with a rational mindset, grounding myself in prayer. I told myself that injustice happens every day, on small and large scales, to everyone around us. One person could be making less money than another in the same job; someone might be on the brink of losing their home due to predatory lending; someone could lose a promotion to someone else who is far less qualified; and, of course, an individual may lose a court case even though they were innocent.

Embracing the fact that life isn't always fair helped me achieve my emotional recovery so that I find myself in a much better position to deal with the unfairness.

This summary of the key facts affected how my case was handled and decided. Before being stuck with this terrible injustice, I had been living as a respectable and honored veteran who was dedicated to serving my country. When I finally got out of the Brig, even though I expressed my concerns and frustrations with many people who could help, I only received apologies, empathy, and sympathies. Many people believe that my case, rather than being subjected to true legal matters, became entangled in a web of poor politics. These were ever-voted public servants under the sun in my direct chains, and some were not. I started with my Mayor and worked my way through Congress and the Senate. I then contacted every appropriate Inspector General and those who would be responsible for the various oversight committees, including the speaker of the House of the time, the Armed Forces Committee members and even those various Intelligence-related oversight committees because they were all relevant in my case. Sharing my message did help others, but I have never personally received any relief at all.

Yet, I haven't and will not lose hope. As part of my war against UCI, in 2021, I appeared at the public meeting of the

Defense Advisory Committee on Investigation, Prosecution, and Defense of Sexual Assault in the Armed Forces (DAC-IPAD). The purpose of DAC-IPAD is to advise the Secretary of Defense on the investigation, prosecution, and defense of allegations of sexual assault and other sexual misconduct involving members of the armed forces.

I was the first person ever in the history of this UCI to request to speak as a victim of injustice who has not been granted relief and is still in a status of "guilty." I was given five minutes to comment on my case and submit documentation. During that time, I explained how I was convicted of sexual assault in 2014 and was sentenced to three years of confinement. I expressed my purpose for seeking justice and even shared a proposal I envisioned, which was a conviction relief unit like the Falsely Accused Individual Review (FAIR) Act, something similar to what the British parliament has and to emphasize the need to permanently commission such a review committee in the interest of all service members and military justice. The military justice system had violated my Constitutional rights, as defined by the commission, and those of many other accused individuals, and I appealed to the committee to review my case and those of others.

Upon initially learning that the Defense Advisory Committee was willing to hear me, I telephoned two others who were suffering from similar injustices and were also able to share their stories. One of whom turned down a presidential pardon because that only restores rights under the premise that one is actually guilty. The other, much like me, was out to seek truth and find as many people as possible who had been affected by the military justice system of the time, much like myself. I didn't see it clearly at the time because I did not know how I, myself, or the others would be received at the event, but I knew there were, at a minimum, several thousand others out there who had been served injustice from my work with various non-profits that were working hard to sound the alarm and bring reason back to the services legal system. I prayed on it, and it just felt like these two gentlemen and I were meant to state our cases that day in a compelling way to initiate change. As a matter of fact, one of them had to travel across the country like me and was facing one obstacle after another getting in his way of making the event, so much so that he texted me, "The enemy is trying to keep me from being there." I simply replied something to the nature of not letting the enemy have its way, and I offered prayers.

At the meeting, I didn't know what would be said because initially, I felt a certain reserve to speak about the topic because it's an intimate topic. I didn't truly want to talk about it or put myself out there, so to speak, but I knew with the faith of a mustard seed it was possible that after we spoke and initiated the era of the victims not acknowledged, others would come forward. Although many are still hesitant, many have and will continue to come forward. There had been a key to the door of justice and relief, and had I been too fearful to pick up the key and open the door, the changes that have occurred may have never occurred. As a man of faith,

I can only describe this as the Good Lord reaching out and guiding me to share the light.

During this meeting, I suggested that the proposed conviction relief unit should review certain integral parameters. One of them was the fact that the armed forces had faced the largest account of Unlawful Command Influence (UCI) in US history. What occurred could be explained as a series of events disregarding service members' rights to fit an agenda enabled by UCI. To elaborate on this, I went on to point out how false accusations relating to sexual assault reached their peak in 2014, precisely when I was convicted. I also mentioned how UCI accounts of the mid-1960s and mid-1980s were nowhere close to the levels that surfaced during my time in the military, yet they produced a plan for the relief of those affected and acted accordingly.

To truly convey the issue, I had to address the committee with all the facts as I knew them. I personally didn't hesitate to name the entities involved in exerting UCI, including the US president, SECDEF, congressional officials, service leaders, the JAG Corps, jury pools, and service members of every armed force who used training, briefings, policy memos, colleague letters, and various other valid and invalid means to influence court-martials at the time. Here, I discussed how the Judge Advocate Generals of the Navy and Air Force, who are expected to embody the spirit of justice, even personally interceded in cases, showing how deeply UCI had penetrated the system.

For my case specifically, I mentioned how the plaintiff and their trial counsel came up with conflicting information and claims at different hearings, and yet the UCI agenda pervaded due to the mismanagement of sexual assault cases by the procession of the armed forces. I also stated that my case was presented to civilian authorities, but since there was no evidence of a crime being committed, they chose to drop the case before it was picked up by the Navy military justice system in 2014, nearly two years later after a thorough investigation involving many law enforcement entities occurred and could find no evidence of a crime.

Something important to note here is that when the justice system wants to cause you harm, they will stack accusations against a person to ensure something can be proven, and they get their win. Oddly, after all the time and resources used in investigating my case, there was only one charge that had to meet several criteria. To me, this shows a clear sign of arrogance. Someone who knew they could get away with just about anything in those courtrooms but was also overly narcissistic to believe they could prove the impossible. In reading the charge sheet and knowing the outcome, in hindsight, it should be noted that whoever this person was, they held and potentially still holds a law license and was and quite possibly still be incredibly dangerous. It was either not a good person or a collective of terrible people.

In the end, apart from advocating a review of my case, I tried to highlight how ridiculous and absurd my conviction was by pointing out that after two years of investigation, the military judge found me guilty for a single statement, according to the star witness I made; "Don't worry, I used a condom." I highlighted how this statement, which was never made, was the whole premise for my conviction and was somehow seen as evidence for no consent. I even showcased that the original statement was different and likely more accurate to her agenda before I suppose she was coached, and at a minimum, it was made so close to the time of the alleged incident that it was more likely to be the true statement made.

That was my submission at the DAC-IPAD.

Seeing the result of my case and how it has been handled, it's clear that the true tragedy was the chain of command that 'framed' a crime from nowhere and set up the conviction. Not only did this massive UCI conduct ruin my career and send me to prison for a crime I did not commit, but it also put me into a never-ending state of mental and emotional distress. And despite striving and fighting for my rights over the past decade, I see no real avenue for relief for me personally because they would finally be acknowledging they were wrong. I even called the judge of my case, who is a judge outside of the military, and asked him if he truly believed he was right about my case, and astonishingly, after a decade, he remembered me and my case, although we had only seen each other for what would equate to a workday during court martial trial he said he stood by his decision. Now, think rationally here. Is It really viable that after all these years and cases he has seen, he would remember details of my case, an alleged one-line "don't worry, I used a condom" statement sealing my fate and standing by a conviction even after the much larger UCI problem was finally being addressed? Absolutely not. There's a good reason he remembers my case, but I highly doubt he will ever reveal why, and if he did, it likely wouldn't be honest after what I have learned and witnessed.

Thinking back to the firepower others had in the form of hot shot attorneys, endless amounts of money, media support, and even political support to have in their corner to get their cases overturned to find justice meant that for me, this is and will be a truly a David and Goliath story. I am not sure how my story will end, but I do know that I am equipped with the heart of David, so I will continue to face my giant for the sake of all affected by this era of injustice.

My goal is to advocate my own path for relief because there currently isn't one for anyone in my status, and if I prevail, others will have a way, too. All of the other veterans who have faced similar damages of injustice but found no clear path to redemption will have one. That is my purpose and my dream here.

As mentioned, I connected with many military prosecutors and defense lawyers of today, all of whom confidently stated that a case like this one would never be pursued presently. That change in the guidance and culture in itself would be enough to prevent many in the future, but what about those who were failed by the system?

Yet, I and many other veterans continue to suffer and are penalized in life. It's high time a FAIR committee is formed that works like a conviction integrity project that ensures that everybody's rights are respected and victims and accused alike are supported. However, to function effectively and ensure that career self-preservation doesn't influence the process of justice, the committee should be composed of a diverse collection of legal professionals who are highly unlikely to be corrupt.

Potentially a mix of non-reservist and non-active-duty military members, collegiate lawyers, and Federal Judges without military ties. Now that we have seen what the weaponization of justice clearly looks like and have observed absolute corruption of the military justice system, we have a new hope in getting things right in the future, but if I and others like me are never granted relief and restoration, then corruption has won.

On the one hand, the purpose of sharing all this information is to let Americans understand the dirty injustices I have had to bear and to work relentlessly to attempt to redeem my namesake, while on the other, I also march forward to, fortunately, have assisted in the prevention of similar instances of injustice from happening to military service members in the past and will hold a continued faith in the future.

Amid the implementation of the UCI agenda, a lot of misinformation has been created that has been causing damage for over a decade. Yet, I believe that there's still time to take corrective actions and make progress toward a path where none are left behind. I truly hope that the effort contributes enough to protect the fate of prospective US Armed Service members and help me recover mine.

Chapter 4: The Court Martial

"The Constitution is the guide which I will never abandon."

That quote made famous by the Founding Father of America, George Washington, is one quote that I now carry deeply in my heart. Primarily because without it, we have no individual rights. Had those who swore an oath to be the defenders of the Constitution against all enemies, foreign and domestic, not allowed for the UCI environment to manifest, relief could have been as easy as an apology and an Honorable - Medical Retirement for me.

It was January 14th, 2014, when I first received a charge sheet from my command that opened up a pandora's box of failed, inaccurate information and unlawful orders related to sexual assaults, including remarks by President Obama. Again, the reason the President is so important in this is because, aside from written orders, he says the service leaders can take anything and everything as a direct order. For those leaders, by this time, the propaganda of training personnel on what constituted sexual assault had spread throughout the United States Armed Forces was probably near 100 percent due to training trackers and how extensive training is mandated and managed. It's true that the repetitive unit training events were pretty concerning, but since they didn't directly impact me at the time, I never allowed them to reach the top of my mind.

When I first went through the charge sheet, what immediately came to my mind was that this was some sort of a sick joke, given that I was only days away from my end-of-service commitment and was soon heading back home to Texas. As a tradition in the military, when a new service member joins or an existing one transfers commands, those who they work with will do something that's not very charming, to say the least. It can be an unfriendly 'hello,' hazing, or paying dues, but whatever they are, they aren't desirable.

It turns out the charge sheet wasn't a joke, and unfortunately, everything I had known to be true would soon be flipped upside down. Little did I know that the sheet was only the beginning of what would result in the most traumatic event in my life, something that would cause me to lose trust in almost everything and just about everyone. I was going to face something that taught me two greatest lessons: First, to lean on faith and willpower and fight with all my ability to change the things that could be changed, and second, to accept things that I could not change as they were at the time.

I was well aware of my innocence in the case, so I was confident that there should be more evidence in my favor than against me. As a result, I carried on with my life without letting the accusation bother me much, especially when I was already stressed with concerns associated with making a career change, selling a house, packing everything, and leaving the place I had spent my 20s, the best decade of my life. As I reflected on the great memories that I had made away from home, it was an emotional time for me, to say the least.

Hence, it took time before I ultimately realized that the charge sheet wasn't part of some sick command hazing hoax and that it was something more serious. A critical occurrence that's worth mentioning here is that my Command Master Chief called me in his office. It was this odd time when the civilians had indefinitely dropped charges against me due to lack of evidence.

I guessed that he wanted to follow up with me on how I was doing with the bunch of other concurrent hardships I was facing. Apart from the sexual assault charge itself, I had just lost my cousin in a tragic accident and had lost several very good friends. I had faced extreme hindering injuries in an accident during a military training pipeline, which resulted in several surgeries and medical problems that would take over three years to heal and return me to a new version of normal. On top of that, I had just broken up with my significant other, someone with whom I had committed to a long-term relationship. If that wasn't enough, our command was also subject to some highly disturbing activities, including a sudden murder, among other things, leaving the command in a traumatic psychological state. They even had sessions with the head Psychiatrist, who briefed them on different ways to cope with grief and other tragedies that had surfaced nearly bi-monthly. This was highly unusual for any Command.

Surprisingly, though, none of these things were mentioned by my Command Master Chief during the session. Instead, it happened to be a trash-talking session toward me, stripping me of my recently hard-earned Expeditionary Warfare Device (EXW) uniform pin, which would be my third. He also mentioned that he was almost done with his Associate degree and that he knew I was merely a recent college graduate earning an Associate degree in the field of Intelligence Operations as well as a Bachelor's degree which was a Bachelors of business administration (B.B.A) with a focus In Technology Management, and planning to apply again for Naval Officer and Coast Guard Commissioning programs. As outrageous as it gets, he bluntly stated that all my efforts toward education were 'pointless because I would never use them.' It all sounded like he invited me to his office to let me know he was going to ensure that I was prosecuted. Clearly, he wanted me to feel like a disabled, broken, and trying-to-recover sailor who would soon be a defendant in a UCI-fueled court-martial. However, I later found out that the command had many of these accusations, and unfortunately, I was the one who took the fall because I had made the conscious decision to transition from enlisted Navy.

As I learned more and more about the sexual assault agenda, Unlawful Command Influence (UCI), and misinformation, including what applied specifically to me, I realized that the rules were less significant. I wanted to know how all of this would affect me, an innocent man, so I first sought civilian counsel, meeting a highly recommended yet expensive attorney in Virginia. This lawyer was straightforward, telling me the cold truth about the deeper agenda and how it could impact me going forward, and gave no cold promises. Even though I was concerned, I still viewed myself in a much stronger position in the case, so I failed to grasp his stance, especially when I was expected to pay a hefty fee. I told him, "Sir, are you telling me that even though it's highly likely that any evidence will be in my favor, and I know with 100% accuracy that I am innocent, just because the congress and military leadership has created an unreasonable environment, I will need to pay you a significant amount of money, and yet, you can't, with any degree of probability, say how successful we will be?" With that comment, I shook his hand and left his office. While it felt like I was being forced into something that wouldn't work out in my favor, I now wish, in hindsight, that I hired the attorney.

After meeting with the civilian attorney, I began exploring representation offered by the Navy JAG (Navy Judge Advocate General) Corps via the Navy Legal System. Most military JAG counsel that I met gave me the impression that the case doesn't sound that serious, telling me to return to them if the justice system decides to even go forward with it. That went on for quite some time. It may have been three or four months, but it felt like forever when your contract was completed and all my personal life responsibilities needed to be taken care of to transition back to home, Texas. These responses aligned perfectly well with my own views at the time and were more promising, too, in terms of how favorable the outcome would be. Their views further confirmed that I made the right decision by not hiring the civilian attorney who had acted more seriously in the case. Boy, were they all wrong.

Other than the fact that the civilian attorney appeared to possess a much better understanding of what was going on, there were other reasons I should have hired him. For one, as a civilian attorney, he wouldn't have been part of the internal JAG core games. Instead, he would have come with added oversight, serving as a public eye, looking into what the military is doing, and reporting anything unjust. Second, at any point in time, he wouldn't have to worry about promotion appeasing someone or following any unlawful orders that were later to be hashed out. Third, he would earn from me rather than being paid by the taxpayers via the government, so they would have worked genuinely in my interests throughout the course of the case.

I ended up hiring a Navy legal JAG. Over time, more paperwork came in, and the interviews with the JAG got lengthier, but they clearly lacked substance. For some reason, his attitude started changing, and interviews felt like I wasn't a sailor exercising my right to defense counsel but an enemy combatant in an interrogation. To this day, I have no idea where his Jekyll and Hyde attitude stemmed from, but I knew that this guy was talented, so I assumed that it might be his way of trying to discover the truth while representing me or there could be some other reason that I was unaware of. He also did exhibit great intellect in all of the proceedings leading up to the court-martial. But at a point when ball control became more important than ever, he dropped it.

During the early interviews with the JAG, he looked like a great talent who had all his stuff together. It seemed to me that he was working hard enough to get me home, so much so that I got mentally ready to see my family. After all, I was far past my end-of-service date. The JAG made me feel so comfortable with the process that I chose not to inform any of my family members or friends about what I was facing. But then my JAG attorney had surgery. That's when his attitude and conversations with me took a turn. I began feeling that he was representing less of me and more of another master, the UCI. Thereafter, every decision he made seemed to have been inspired by a UCI playbook.

This change in behavior on my JAG's part compelled me to call home and explain to my family that I had a case pending in which I was being represented by a Navy JAG. I also told them that although I knew I was innocent, my concern came from the process and that the process seemed to be taking a turn in the wrong direction. The call was also to let them know I would request them to participate and observe how the case was unfolding by getting them to court-martial if they decided to allow it to go that far. They recommended I connect with Carl Parker, who was a lawyer and had been a Navy JAG and Texas Senator back around the time of J.F. Kennedy. I did call and speak to him but mentioned that I knew my innocence would stand my ground, and this I believed would itself work in my favor. I said that I strongly believed that everything should be okay. I also told him that I would call him if things got too out of hand.

It was only when my JAG attorney lost at the court-martial that I realized that things did slip out of my hands, after which I requested Mr. Parker's professional assistance. He tried to contact various people in authority and issued a brief, raising an objection that the case didn't have enough evidence to lead to a guilty verdict. UCI was not over yet, so the response by the Admirals and the Convening authority was, "He still has appeals left, and our JAG Corps is here to ensure his rights are protected and justice is served." Once again, they couldn't have been more wrong, and the UCI power struck and had me right where the playbook wanted me. Following this response, a military appeal attorney who was considered the best in the US was hired, but it's important to note here that hired attorneys in appeal are always secondary to the military attorneys that are originally assigned. In addition, one of the most daunting realities that I noted in my own case was that when you tried seeking help from a civilian attorney, the military staff assigned to you would lose nearly all interest in you to a point where they would stop answering your phone calls, letters, and questions for lengthy periods. Even when they're available, they'd be of no help at all.

I was not the only one facing injustice, though. When I was being prosecuted, another Senior Chief Navy Seal was facing similar, UCI-triggered charges. After years of fighting appeals and sitting in the Brig, we noted a retired Admiral making public statements that accused the Legal Corps officials of allowing politics and public relations concerns to dictate the outcomes of court martials. According to the admiral, the Navy Judge Advocate General (JAG) exerted UCI by attempting to convince the Navy not to vindicate the sailor and to prevent the Navy's image from being tarnished. The statement inarguably shows how powerful and influential UCI was at the time, precisely when I was court-martialed. It was extremely unlikely that another Convening Authority or Admiral would get so bold about it. In that case, the Supreme Court of Armed Forces found that the top Navy JAG, including Vice Admiral James Crawford III and Vice Admiral Nanette DeRenzi, contributed to UCI.

This presented more proof of the UCI environment in which my case was being handled. Yet, not a single person raised the argument in my favor, even when there was more than enough to work from. I also experienced some bad luck, as additional evidence that could have strengthened my case against UCI—such as phone records—didn't come to light until my appeals were complete. It's important to note that phone records are usually one of the first types of evidence pursued by law enforcement in an investigation.

Unfortunately, I have reached a stage where the avenues for relief are limited to seeking a presidential pardon. As of January 2, 2024, I was denied the opportunity to ask questions or receive any information regarding how the determinations were made. As an innocent party, it's incredibly disturbing to know that my ability to prove my innocence rests solely on the option of a pardon. The entire purpose of the legal system is to establish guilt, and they clearly have not done so in my case. However, I did not realize that I was defending my innocence from day one. This is a true paradigm shift of justice, especially to legal professionals who know you can't prove innocence, and is why prosecutors must prove guilt beyond a reasonable doubt, with emphasis on beyond.

Many legal officials who review my case today agree that given the evidence presented against me, I should have pleaded not guilty, and the case should have been over much earlier. If you were to look back at all the appeals and arguments of the period, you would have a clear idea of the kind of injustice I have experienced in the past decade. Not only were my constitutional rights violated, but there was also nothing impartial or fair during any stage of the trial. The entire case, dragged by a series of UCI instances, was and still serves as a disgrace to justice everywhere. As Dr. Martin Luther King Jr. stated:

"Injustice anywhere is a threat to justice everywhere."

And he was absolutely correct when it comes to individual rights.

Strangely, my court martial session lasted half a day, even though most would last weeks or at least the majority of a week or more.

The Details of My Trial:

The trial commenced with a charged atmosphere, as the government side was eager to secure a conviction against me. Now, allow me to outline the narrative they wove against me during the proceedings. Remember, as you read this section, this is only what they were pushing as a narrative, and it is not supported by facts or evidence.

In their opening statement, the prosecution claimed that Lance Corporal H. overheard me uttering the words, "Don't worry, I used a condom," while allegedly forcing myself upon her when she was in a semi-conscious state. They argued that I ordered drinks for her with the intention of assaulting her while she was drunk. According to their narrative, she consumed three shots with me at a bar, becoming extremely intoxicated to the point where she couldn't walk and had limited awareness of her surroundings. She only remembered waking up next to me in the morning, covered in an unfamiliar sticky substance, prompting her to take a bath.

During the shower, she noticed bite marks on her body, causing her to panic and hastily leave the bathroom. She wrapped a towel around herself, left her clothes to dry in the dryer, and waited briefly until they were ready. After that, she dressed herself, walked out of my apartment, spotted a taxi, and decided to take it. To strengthen their argument, the prosecution presented that very taxi driver as a witness. The driver testified that she sensed that Lance Corporal H. was intoxicated and appeared disheveled, leading her to believe something harmful had happened. Offering her assistance, she proposed taking the Lance Corporal to the police station. The Lance Corporal, visibly upset and disoriented, denied the offer, further hindering her credibility, which in any other court in the United States would have been highly favorable for impeaching the witness and letting me go a free man. This was not good for the prosecution's case.

Among all of the things that are blatantly manifested from thin air, the taxi driver and the Lance Corporal actually threw their own wrench in the allegations of the prosecution when they both testified she did not, in fact, request nor was interested in being brought to the police for help.

Furthermore, the prosecution produced physical evidence: two used condoms found near my apartment. According to the report, the DNA analysis matched both mine and the Lance Corporal's DNA, leading them to assert my guilt.

Again, what that confirms is that sex either occurred or was attempted. These "condom police" evidently think used condoms mean sexual assault. Let's take a second to think rationally here. Two condoms, sexually related activities, and that means sexual assault? Absolutely not.

However, my lawyer effectively challenged the prosecution's claims. He argued that the evidence presented did not even merely indicate an assault and did not prove the presence of forceful sex without consent. He clarified that the drinks in question were simply a single shot and two pineapple-based drinks, which may not have significantly impaired the alleged victim's ability to consent. Moreover, he was prepared to call upon Dr. Moore, an expert witness, to explain to the court the concept of blackouts. Unfortunately, this subject matter expert was never called to the stand because my defense thought that it was unnecessary because the government had no case and no real evidence.

Furthermore, my lawyer questioned the government's evidence regarding how the alleged victim ended up in my apartment. He pointed out the absence of any witnesses to prove that I had taken her there or forcefully brought her there. He also raised doubts about the evidence demonstrating that the alleged victim was substantially incapable of giving consent. My lawyer even refuted the claims about the sticky substance found on the alleged victim's body, which, when Army CID Investigated, was nonexistent. He challenged the prosecution to provide concrete evidence to support their assertions. Clearly, they did not, and personally, I knew they could not because when you're innocent, you are innocent regardless of how someone feels. Courts are for law, period.

During the course of the trial, my lawyer successfully uncovered gaps in the government's case. He demonstrated that they were unable to provide the necessary proof to support any of their claims. The threshold for a conviction is beyond a reasonable doubt, which means that if any doubt is left after all the evidence has been presented, the ruling is supposed to be not guilty. After what they presented, the only thing left for anyone to conclude could be nothing but doubt. Therefore, in a just courtroom, reaching beyond a reasonable doubt was impossible: a conviction.

While in trial, my lawyer raised several questions regarding the actions of Lance Corporal H. in the unfamiliar apartment. He questioned the plausibility of her decision to take a bath in such a confusing and distressing situation. He pointed out the peculiar nature of her behavior, including the alleged act of writing a message on the foggy bathroom mirror, stating, "I'm in hell, help me!" When asked about this, Lance Corporal H. provided no explanation and appeared to avoid answering the question directly.

My lawyer highlighted her habit of speaking in a low voice, at times making her responses inaudible through the microphone. Even during the preliminary hearings prior to the court-martial, when the military judge or my defense would ask questions through the use of technology, the phone would mute to consult her attorney on how to respond. I am sorry to say this, but if you need an attorney to tell you what happened according to your own story, that is a clear indicator of either lying or coaching the witness, in my opinion. Due to our locations during the earlier hearings that led to the court-martial, The phones were muted, and sidebar conversations occurred, where every action was recorded. However, nobody will ever know what those silent conversations were really about. My best guess was that it was coached by her Special Victims Counsel, who acted as a barrier between her and everyone, even her own assigned prosecuting attorney.

Despite these challenges, we persevered in questioning her. We even raised doubts about Lance Corporal H.'s familiarity with the layout of my apartment. Not only did she claim to have taken a shower, but she also allegedly found the dryer and patiently waited while her clothes dried, all while wrapped in a towel. We found it necessary to question how she could have known the ins and outs of the apartment to such an extent and be so "at home" while also stating she did not come in contact with me that morning.

Additionally, my lawyer sought clarification from Lance Corporal H. regarding any morning encounters she may have had with me. While she initially denied any contact, she later attempted to support her story by suggesting that she could hear my voice without being able to see me. However, considering the submitted diagram of my small apartment, her claim of roaming around in my apartment, from taking a shower to waiting for her clothes to dry, all while not seeing me but hearing my voice, appeared unlikely.

This is where things get extremely confusing for me because I was there, and while her clothes dried, she came and sat by me on the sofa, dropped her towel, and began a continuance of what occurred earlier that morning coming from the bar.

These questioning tactics were aimed at challenging the credibility and consistency of Lance Corporal H.'s account, as well as shedding doubt on the feasibility of some of the events described.

During the trial, my lawyer even expressed doubt about how she managed to find a cab immediately after leaving my apartment. He called upon the government to provide substantial evidence to support their seemingly fictional claims. This was disproven by testimony from the taxi driver, who stated that a male with my phone number was the person who called and requested the taxi for her. Even mentioned that she was on the phone with me while we gathered the Lance Corporals' things, to the extent of me coming to the door and letting her know she would be right out so she could put her clothes on as the taxi arrived a little sooner than expected.

We brought attention to Lance Corporal H.'s visit to the 7-Eleven, where she purchased a soda and cigarettes. He questioned how someone who was supposedly distraught and confused, as the government claimed, could be in the mood for a soda. He raised concerns about inconsistencies in Lance Corporal H.'s behavior, which brazenly deviated from their narrative.

Our side also raised questions about the lack of evidence regarding the supposed marks on her body that the government referred to. We highlighted how Lance Corporal H. went to a pre-scheduled medical facility appointment the day after the alleged assault yet failed to mention any signs of marks or assault to the doctor. We questioned how it was possible for her to have never seen me but still hear my voice while simultaneously denying that she heard me speaking to her.

Her delayed visit to the medical facility and the concealment of the sexual assault raised suspicion. We tried to inquire about her behavior, but she repeatedly claimed ignorance or lack of memory regarding most of the questions raised. There were more than enough inconsistencies between her previous testimonies and her statements in court during the cross-examination to have her impeached at a minimum and, at most, put behind bars.

During the trial, the prosecution attempted to address the inconsistencies in their story by asserting that Lance Corporal H. was heavily intoxicated and under the influence of substances, which impaired her cognitive abilities. They argued that her confusion and helplessness prevented her from effectively expressing herself, suggesting that her only means of communication was through the mirror message.

The prosecution built their case around sympathy, emphasizing Lance Corporal H.'s alleged state of intoxication and claiming that she was unable to recall any details due to the substance that was allegedly introduced into her drink. They attempted to justify their claims of vomit and urine based on the alleged level of intoxication in her body.

Note that we had the drug screening and labs from the doctor's visit as evidence that there were no drugs nor alcohol in her system, and the prosecution knew this, and still, he preceded to proclaim this narrative to the judge alone as we did not choose a panel because of the UCI environment.

In response, my lawyer challenged these assertions, questioning how someone could be so intoxicated that they could not remember events from the previous week, such as the dinner that she allegedly had with me. Furthermore, my lawyer raised the question of why Lance Corporal H. chose to visit a 7-Eleven instead of seeking help from the police station or a hospital. All of this was going well until they decided to play dirty.

The trial took an unexpected turn when the prosecution sought to place blame on us, suggesting that my lawyer had taken advantage of Lance Corporal H.'s intoxicated state. They insinuated that the liquid found on her body that morning was likely sexual fluids, arguing that such an outcome could not occur with consensual sex, which is an absurd statement to make by anyone who has ever had sex. They also highlighted Lance Corporal H's delay in reporting the assault, attributing it to fear of reporting me and asking the court to consider her mental turmoil after going through such a traumatic experience.

In conclusion, the prosecution presented a less than compelling case against me, meticulously prepared with somewhat supporting evidence that we had sex, but nothing of ill or malicious intent. However, my defense team diligently challenged their claims into oblivion, even to the extent that the testimony of the Lance Corporal was so questionable and inconsistent that it was sufficient enough to impeach her as a witness, which the judge denied, and demanded concrete evidence of non-consensual sexual acts. Despite refuting their allegations and providing logical reasoning, the judge ultimately reached a verdict against me.

To this day, not one single independent judge, lawyer, commander, conservative nor democratic congressman, conservative nor democratic senator, or person, after reading the court transcript, has concluded on their own has even attempted to justify the judge's decision.

What is important to consider about this is that before God and the spirit of justice, the prosecution crossed the lines and speculated possibilities as if they were telling a fairy tale and not things that actually were supported by evidence. The only evidence they had was her testimony against me, which was rattled with inconsistencies or blatant lies.

I know because I was there through the whole experience as well, and nearly every detail was manipulated in such a way as to give the prosecutor hope to "win." When the prosecution's narrative didn't work out, it was now clearly the strategic forgetfulness and "I don't know" replies during questioning. Had they been answered directly, I would have flipped the government's witness from against me to clear my name. When I say government witness, that is because when you look into my case, you will not find the origin of an accusation, and it became overly apparent that my accuser was the government and not the person.

Upon hearing the judge's conclusion of finding out guilty, where before I had felt no fear, my body went into such a state of disgust that I began gagging uncontrollably and vomited in the trash can next to me.

Chapter 5: The Brig Façade

"You are here as punishment, not to be further punished."

This is a quote that everyone who enters a military prison, also known as a Brig, hears repeatedly from guards, counselors, and other staff. However, it couldn't be farther from the truth. It comes directly from the concept of confinement as a tool of criminal justice known as "doing time." Yes, the punishment is taking away freedoms of your own time. That is the punishment, the time. Yet as one goes through the process of being indoctrinated into this new, terrible, and hopefully temporary way of life, they eventually make their way to the repetition of Groundhog Days that Einstein would describe as insanity, had he expected a different outcome than insanity itself. That is doing the same thing every single day, expecting no different results. Wake up at 5, have four or five inspections a day, eat three times, have some time to read, write, or play spades, have an hour to exercise if weather and staffing permitted, and shower before bed. The same thing happens every day, for years, and for some a lifetime.

During the time of change, that statement about punishment became less meaningful as it initially gets verbally contradicted by the warden over the entire Brig, who comes in and introduces himself to you and says, "My policy is wack-a-mole. Try and rise up in any way, and I'll make sure you're smacked right back down." After hearing that and still dealing with the shock of unjustly having to serve time in a Brig, we all start to look around and wonder what the heck is really going on or about to go on. What does "rising up" even mean? Obviously, we aren't there to take over the Brig, so what the heck did the Wardens' words really mean?

As time went on, we would learn what it really meant, and it meant that, for the most part, they could smack you down in their own ways whenever they wanted, and mostly without repercussions. Taking privileges earned such as access to the library or "library call," weight room, unjustified negative counseling, repeated unnecessary inspections, which when I mention any inspection, we were standing at full attention for 45 minutes to over an hour sometimes up to five times a day. Even worse, they would use the medical staff against you if you used the required medicine so they could ensure you "felt the pain" if those staff members felt like it. Things were quite bad for a while until some finally had the fortitude to do the right thing and make formal outside reports while also expecting that some form of reprisal would follow. One primary person was me, and there were a few others that I would not name at this time. It was so bad that they had policy posters on the wall next to the telephones that charge fifty cents a minute, which gave a number to the Inspector General (IG) to report serious issues such as prison rape and any other terrible thing under the sun.

One day, after gathering enough information, I finished my own personal investigation and realized a laundry list of things that were all a façade. Being as I had something important to report and willingly accepted any consequences that would follow, I picked up the phone and dialed the number to the Inspector General only to find out that it didn't work. Not in my dorm or any dorm. Our literal only way to make legitimate reports was not real. This led to them shuffling me around and starting to act like real professionals, being that the Inspector General doesn't take reports lightly and ensures you are first safe, away from prying ears, and that nobody knows you are making an IG complaint. Unfortunately, since the hotline was a façade, people knew I had made a complaint, which led to the IG finally visiting the site and interviewing prisoners. As I expected, I was reprised against, which was investigated by an IG investigator with no name, just an identifying number for credentials and safety, who found the reprisal truthful but also added, "Without a name, I cannot proceed." So essentially, nobody was willing to dime the Brig terrorist out, and the case was closed with missing Information.

My entry into the Brig was immediately from court martial. They brought me to the back of the building and hauled me away in a van. I had no idea this would happen, so at the time, I was still in shock while also trying to focus on accepting the current realities of those moments. It was quite strange because one of the guys in the van who would turn me into the Brig was a guy from work, and on the hour or so trip, he was speaking in parables to me about how he went to the Brig because he had some sort of mental issues. Outside of the courtroom, this was the first lie in a long series of lies that would mirror some sort of individually targeted psychological operation. I mostly ignored the tales being told, but it made me wonder what his goal was.

Arriving at the Brig was, of course, strange to someone who had never experienced something like this was another stressful event in a totally separate series of suck. They process you, have someone come give you a mental health assessment, and leave you in a cold, lonely cell for up to days until they get you to the second stage of processing. While being moved to this small area, some refer to as "the hole," I started to have chest pains and couldn't breathe, so I had physiological responses and asked the medical person who was responding to me to check me out and do an EKG, or anything to figure out what was going on and if I would be ok. The medical chief put an EKG on me that had no batteries for power and just let me sit there on the table in pain until hours passed and my body stabilized. It was so terrible I honestly thought I was dying. However, as I recovered and they put me back solitary in my cell in the "hole," a day went by. Putting first things first, I tried to keep my body from overreacting, which was difficult given I was an innocent man living this new life and had no idea what to expect.

I began the first calm day, and I didn't feel the insanity by actually eating and observing what was around through the serving tray slot. You could hear things and kind of make out what was going on from time to time until they felt comfortable enough with you to let you out of your cell and sit either outside, known as a "sunshine call," or clean a small common area with other people who were soon to be processed to their next living quarters known to everyone as "hold"; where people who are on hold for trial were kept.

As I continued to try to understand this environment, I had been sitting in a cell for a few days without being let out and without the medications that I require, and my tinnitus in those concrete walls was terrible, so I wasn't doing too well, and not doing much that a rock couldn't do until one of the guards came around and said: "would you like to go to sunshine call?" I sounded back, still confused and asked, "What's a sunshine call?" The guard said it was where you get to go outside for a little while. At that point, I was fairly happy to hear that and agreed to participate in the sunshine call until he brought me to the back door of an area that looked like a dog kennel. I asked what I should do, just stand in a small area of the fence because there was nothing to sit on. His reply was simply, "yeah". I immediately turned, looked at the Guard, and said, "This isn't for me; I'd rather be in that hole inside." Then we went. Ironically, my first day being processed in the Brig was July 4th weekend. I mean, what a slap in the face, right? Almost like it was planned that way for me to celebrate our country's freedom from tyranny in a military prison.

Since I had already been tried and wasn't awaiting trial, they would soon process me into long-term holding. It was much like "hold" with more options and being treated somewhat more humanely. Regarding day-to-day operations or the never-ending groundhog days of cleaning, we were persistently harassed, and in some ways, I would classify the activity as torture. It's not your average, everyday stuff you don't want to do; it was legitimate torture.

Confined within the cold walls of a military detention center located in Chesapeake, Virginia, my days were engulfed in a relentless nightmare. Years stolen from my life, each day a relentless assault on my senses and spirit. As I recall that harrowing ordeal, fear, anger, and a desperate yearning for justice, an abundance of emotions still churns within me.

Within the confines of the military detention facility, there was this one group of guards whom everyone called the "Goon Squad." Their reputation preceded them, a chilling whisper that sent shivers down the spines of even the most hardened inmates. Unlike the weary indifference of the others, the Goon Squad exuded a predatory glint in their eyes, a sadistic pleasure in enforcing the rules with theatrical severity. Their presence sent shockwaves through the ranks of inmates, instilling a sense of fear and apprehension that permeated every corner of the Brig.

My first encounter with the Goon Squad was on my very first day - a day that is forever etched in my memory. Innocent and naive, I was yet to grasp the gravity of my situation. But as I stood face to face with these enforcers of cruelty, a multitude of negative emotions would take over my being. There were times a bunch of us got our cells searched for absolutely no reason at all or something as trivial as cutting the line at chow. They called it a "toss" - a fancy term for a humiliating and invasive search. It was more monotony and injury to insult because we were inspected every single morning, and everything had to be perfect, just like boot camp, bed and clothes folded nicely, all things out in order according to the images of a manual they gave us as reference for standards as well as did a personnel inspection to include ensuring a clean shaved face, and clean uniform before we could leave for breakfast.

While we were away at breakfast, this was the time for the Goon Squad to do whatever they felt like doing to our belongings. With no one watching, they tossed around all our neatly organized things and made a total mess. So we would go eat, just to be on our way back with a knot in our stomachs, not knowing if the good guards had made our day exponentially harder than it needed to be. This was the case for every time we weren't in the primary dorm room. Even on the days when we were locked down, they would still toss rooms, but we couldn't see what was going on; we just heard the sounds and the stories afterward.

For many of us, if not all of us, it felt like we were being singled out, as if the Goon Squad was making an example of us. The practice of "tossing your room" was a cruel tactic employed to prevent any semblance of progress, in my opinion, but it was justified as a way to ensure there was not any contraband. Contraband could be identified without taking an entire record of trial in order by page numbers and throwing them into the air, leaving a mess to try and recover and organize, as our freedoms in some cases depended on it. Every call was recorded; every letter was monitored—our every move was scrutinized under the watchful eye of the Brig staff and the hatred of the famous Stanford Study-like humans known to us as the Goon Squad.

It was a stark reminder of the harsh reality I now found myself in—a reality where innocence held little sway in the face of unchecked power. Some of the worst memories were from being trapped inside our concrete block cells at night without working air flow or air conditioning. The only way to make it through the night was to turn up the radio, which usually produced only static, to drown out the torture of terrible tinnitus—a constant ringing in the ears from damage. We would pour water on the concrete floor and lie on it, much like a dog splooting to stay cool. The good news was that the cells and floors stayed immaculately clean due to our regimented routine. The heat and floor sleeping were harsh enough on this disabled veteran, but to better understand tinnitus, the CEO of Chik Fil-a ended up with it as a result of covid and couldn't take the noise, which unfortunately resulted in his death by suicide. But the Brig staff didn't care. At most, the groundskeeper and one of the two key enlisted leaders who happened to be Navy Chiefs were the only ears who had any empathy for us in the dorms. Unfortunately, that did not come around too often.

People filed complaints through the official channels, but it felt like a bureaucratic shrug. The investigation report said their claims were unsubstantiated because they waited too long to report them or gave some other excuses. It made all of us feel like they didn't believe us like our experiences didn't matter. The report said the goon squad was just doing their jobs, enforcing the rules. But that's not actuality. It felt like constant harassment that could ruin your day at any time. They seemed to take an immense amount of pleasure in abusing their power.

There was this one Marine, a guy who had served for decades. The goon squad took his journal, the one he used to write about his PTSD. They claimed it was contraband because it had another detainee's information in it. It seemed like a flimsy excuse to me - they were probably just trying to mess with him. They even tried to say he hurt his knee while playing soccer instead of admitting someone had done something to him.

The most frustrating thing was that they never even interviewed any of us about our complaints. It felt like they had already made up their minds that they didn't care about what happened to us. There was this sailor Perkins who said the goon squad roughed him up during a search and called him names. They didn't interview him either, and they dismissed his claims because he waited too long to report them.

The whole system felt overly rigged. We were supposed to be doing "time" as punishment, not be further punished, but how when we were not able to report abuse, they would just ignore our complaints. Perkins was having nightmares and stuff because of what they did to him, but nobody in charge seemed to care. It made you feel like they could get away with anything.

The brig was a terrible experience. It showed me how much power some people have and how little they care about the people they are supposed to be in charge of and keep protected while serving time. The goon squad became a symbol of that unchecked power, a symbol of how cruel people can be. Their actions are something I will never forget.

This whole thing was so messed up. We go through this whole process to report abuse, and then they just act like it never happened.

The relentless grip of solitary confinement squeezed the life out of the days within the brig. Weeks blurred together, each one charged with what appeared to be escalating abuse. Confined in a windowless cell, I felt stripped of my humanity, a caged animal yearning for the warmth of the sun. The bitter winter gnawed at the thin walls, its icy breath seeping through and chilling me to the bone. Huddled in a corner, I prayed for justice that never came.

From the moment I stepped inside that place, the warden's indoctrination began. Their voices, heavy with malice, would pronounce the chilling mantra, "Whack a mole. Rise up, get whacked." This grim warning served as a constant reminder of the absolute authority they wielded, leaving no room for dissent.

But the physical intimidation was merely the tip of the iceberg. A more insidious torment that gnawed at us was the relentless pursuit of guilt, regardless of our innocence. Counseling sessions were nothing different than a battleground, where extracting confessions became their primary objective, and they enjoyed achieving their desired confessions from prisoners' mouths through any means necessary. It was so bad that for a long period of time, I would see a counselor who was actually a Ph.D. and not a social worker or military equivalent whom I would spill my heart out about my experiences and innocence, only to find out that one day she would quit due to her assessment that what was going on at that Brig was awful, and she couldn't handle not being able to do anything to help. Also, the scarcity of mental healthcare within the facility only served to underscore the rigged nature of the system, and there was not even an actual medical doctor on the remote site where we were being held.

These were not counselors or guards; they were psychological tormentors disguised in uniforms or hiding behind titles. They reveled in their power, taunting us with arbitrary commands and subjecting us to degrading inspections. Each day brought a fresh onslaught of humiliation, a deliberate erosion of our self-worth.

Access to mental health professionals was a cruel joke. Inmates were left to silently grapple with their demons as their minds unraveled before our very eyes. Families torn apart and lives shattered by the sheer weight of injustice – these were the true casualties of a system that prioritized punishment over rehabilitation.

One particularly sadistic tactic employed by the guards previously mentioned was the practice of "tossing your room." Again, this meant the complete ransacking of our cells, not an inspection as it was supposed to be. If anything, it acted as a blatant attempt to prevent any progress. Every conversation was recorded; every letter was monitored, and our every move was scrutinized under cameras and the staff's watchful eyes.

One day, a guy who had become a good acquaintance because we shared weightlifting in common had enough, and he was about to let the whole place know. Now, this wasn't your normal lean and mean typical Marines. This guy was a Chesty Puller, "Take me to the Brig so I can meet the real Marines" kind of Marine. Although some of the details are not well remembered, as we worked out one day, I remember him telling me that he had enough of these "p**** a**" people running the Brig and that he was going to show them how weak they were one day. Well, the next day was quite the show. I can't remember where it started, but it ended up with all of the staff on deck, safe away from the marine; they did not chain him as usual but put the facility on lockdown and let him escort himself to the hole, where after a short time he began what seemed like part two of his plan. He slammed and banged as long and loud as he could until the guards were ordered to go into his cell by the duty officer of the day, a Marine Gunnery Sergeant. That, unfortunately, wasn't going to happen, even with all of the gear. This guy was a beast; he knew it and was using it to accomplish his mission. He embarrassed Gunny and showed how weak these people really were.

The last I can recall of that incident was what we heard listening over the guards' radios. The guards were getting nowhere with this Marine, and they knew it, so he plainly said, "Let me talk to Gunny, y'all can't do s***!" The Gunny Sergeant did roger up on the radio, and all we heard was the Gunny avoiding anything confrontational and the Marine making his request at first, and then demanding that since his guards could not do their job, he insisted the Gunny go see him and "handle things." Well, that didn't happen either, as the last we heard over the radio was the Marine calling the Gunny a "Giant P****" who could never be a real leader, and he didn't deserve his attention. Needless to say, that man accomplished his mission. Eventually, he was let out sometime well after this incident, and while working out one day, he told me the rest of the details, but that's his story to tell, not mine.

Despite the despair that threatened to engulf me, I refused to surrender to their cruelty, much like that Marine but in a respectful manner, as I had never been one to play games. I decided to seek help from the higher-ups, naively hoping to get their support. Yet, my desperate pleas for help fell on deaf ears. The very system designed to uphold justice had abandoned me, leaving me adrift in an even deeper sea of injustice.

The story of the coffee bean holds incredible power. I didn't realize it then, but I exercised that power long before I understood it. In the brig, we had a TV schedule that operated on a first-come, first-served basis until everyone was around. Then, it became a matter of votes. On Sundays, I often woke up early and watched whatever was on, not paying much attention because I wasn't invested in voting. But over time, something started to shift in me, and I assume others could see it too.

I had started attending church more often, and my demeanor must have been apparent as I became more grounded. One morning, I woke early and noticed Joel Osteen was on TV. I watched alone, not expecting much. But as I listened, it felt like Joel spoke directly to me. His words of encouragement and inspiration reached into the corners of my soul that I hadn't touched in a long time. It was a small moment, but it meant everything.

Weeks passed, and I continued my routine—waking up early and listening to Joel's messages. Then, something unexpected happened. One by one, others in the brig started joining me. First, it was just one person standing quietly by the TV, then another, and another. Eventually, nobody voted for that time slot anymore. We all either watched or listened to Joel's sermons. I hadn't planned for this, but my decision to seek encouragement somehow created a ripple effect. The environment was changing—subtly at first, but undeniably.

In hindsight, I realized I had become a coffee bean. Like the coffee bean that changes the water it's placed in, I had unknowingly transformed my environment. What started as a private moment of seeking comfort and faith had evolved into a collective experience. Race, color, creed—none mattered. We all woke up to hear Joel at some point, and in doing so, the energy of the brig shifted. People who once never spoke to each other found themselves quietly listening together, sharing in something more profound than our circumstances.

The changes weren't just in what we watched but in how we acted. Conversations became softer, and there was less tension. It was as if Joel's messages were seeping into the fabric of our daily lives, encouraging us to be better to one another. The atmosphere lightened, and in a place where conflict was the norm, we found moments of peace.

This experience sparked an idea in me. If something as simple as being steadfast in watching Joel's sermons could change the environment around me, maybe there was hope for the entire brig. Maybe, with time and patience, the whole place could heal somehow. And so, I made it my mission to keep going and remain committed to this path. Over time, the improvement was undeniable. Joel had brought us all together, helping us heal our wounds and inspiring us to keep moving forward in the name of Jesus.

Looking back, I realize the power to change my environment was within me. Like the coffee bean, I didn't need to force anything. All it took was a quiet commitment to positivity, faith, and inspiration. Through that, I helped spark a slight transformation, and together, we found light in a place where it was hard to see.

Even in the darkest corners, a glimmer of hope flickered inside me. The belief that justice, though delayed, would eventually be prevailed. As I write these words, I do so with a renewed sense of purpose. My story is but one voice in a chorus demanding change. The reign of those terrible people who operate the Brig and the Goon Squad may have left its indelible mark, but it will not define us. We are survivors, bound together by a shared experience and a fierce determination to see accountability.

Chapter 6: A New Stronger Self

"Success is not final, failure is not fatal: it is the courage to continue that counts."

– Winston S. Churchill

By now, you probably have a good idea of what I went through. I will be the first to admit it wasn't easy. At times, I genuinely didn't think I would survive. When everything happens backward, or upside down, one tends to learn to have absolutely no expectations, period. You have to adjust to a whole new world in there, both physically and mentally, just to barely make it. Every day was different, never knowing what to expect. That constant uncertainty was terrifying, like walking into a dark room in which someone set traps. Remembering dark times, for those who understand what I am talking about through experience, I just want to say on the record that watching the movie Shawshank Redemption on the inside is different than on the outside. It's much more than just a movie when you can truly feel what the characters are experiencing as they portray emotions that mirror our own reality. Do not recommend it, but hey, you have been embodied with the power of choice.

After a while, I felt like I was finally getting the hang of things. Two and a half years in, I was even eligible for probation. Remember how I told you about advocating for better conditions for people in civilian prisons and Guantanamo Bay? Well, it felt like they had it way easier than us. They at least had some kind of support system to help them get back on their feet after they got out.

For us, it was almost rigged from the start. They set these outrageously high standards for parole, but they didn't give you the tools you needed to meet them. It was like, "You need a job to get paroled, but you can't get a job if you can't talk to people normally." It just didn't make sense.

Most people ended up stuck because they couldn't meet these impossible requirements. There weren't any programs to help you find work, which might still be the case today. Luckily, I had a family member who owned a business. They could immediately give me a job, which was a huge help.

Here's the thing: I've been out for fourteen years now. Fourteen years, and I haven't gotten into any trouble. That should tell you something, right? I'm a reasonably normal member of society and then a member of the service, not some mischievous criminal. However, they treat everyone the same, applying the same rules to everyone unless you contest them, but not everyone's situation is the same. These rules are built for failure. The system isn't designed to help you succeed but to keep you locked up. I personally went over inmates' case files to learn more while also identifying the rights violations that weren't brought up in hopes of helping navigate the legal lingo, but also to put together pardon packages where I saw clear conflicts of interest and violations of individual rights. It was not only good deeds, but helping others, whoever my opposition working at the institution was, only became more frustrated and gave me hell until the day I left.

Finally, the day came. I was getting paroled. It was hard to believe. Paroled. The word felt strange on my tongue, almost unbelievable after everything I'd been through. My head was a mess after all those years. The guards had messed with me, played mind games, and thrown punishments at me left and right.

It felt unreal. After everything I'd been through, the mental games, the constant punishments for nothing, I was actually walking out of that place.

Remember that warden's motto - "Whack a mole?" Well, I guess I'd been doing alright in there, keeping my head down. Apparently, that wasn't good enough for them. The system seemed to retaliate right around the time I figured things out. Just as I started collecting evidence of all the messed-up stuff going on, the harassment began again. Just because I figured out the system learned the rules, that wasn't good enough. They had to make an example of me.

But I fought back, bit by bit. It wasn't easy, but slowly things started to improve. The constant stress and fear all started to ease up a little. It was a huge change going from being on edge all the time to... well, to freedom.

Leaving that place and returning to the real world was like coming out of a pressure cooker. Always on edge, jumpy, and worried about what was coming next. Could I even handle normal life again? Even on the plane, I couldn't quite believe it was real. I thought to myself, where is this plane even going? For all I knew, it was en route to the Brig in Guantanamo Bay, Cuba.

Walking out of that place and onto the airplane, it still didn't feel real. Truth be told, even on the plane ride, I wasn't sure where I was really going. They tell you they're flying you home to see your probation officer, but after all the lies, who knew what to believe anymore?

Then, when I landed in Texas at the Jack Brooks airport, I saw them. My family. It had been over two years since I'd seen a single familiar face.

That's when it hit me. I was finally home. Even though the terms of my parole were more than shaky, even though I didn't know how long this freedom would last, it didn't matter. Right there, surrounded by my family, I knew I was home.

Coming home, the first thing on my mind was finding a job. This is where most people stumble after getting out. You're labeled a felon, and suddenly, nobody wants to take a chance on you. Luckily, I had a family member who was willing to give me a shot at their company.

It wasn't easy, though. Getting back on your feet means a ton of classes, meetings, and all this stuff that costs money you probably don't have. It felt like the whole system was designed to keep you down, watching you like a hawk for any misstep. All these rules crammed onto these giant papers that made no sense.

But I kept my head down, focused on work and those endless meetings. Even though they weren't much help to me personally, I could see how they might benefit others who were actually struggling with their sins. The whole situation forced me to adapt constantly. There was no one-size-fits-all program for someone like me, someone who ended up a felon over a drink or two with a woman.

Meanwhile, I was surrounded by people facing some serious demons. It put my own problems in perspective. Slowly but surely, I started getting my bearings. Work, home, probation stuff, the never-ending cycle of tests - polygraphs, drug tests, the whole nine yards. Once I had that under control, I could finally start thinking about being social again.

Now, don't get me wrong, I talked to people in the brig and before that, too. I was a very social person who moved to an entirely new region of the US and could almost guarantee there wasn't a place you could go where someone didn't know me. But it wasn't the same. There was always this cloud hanging over me, a feeling of shame about what happened. It felt like a heavy cloak I couldn't take off, making even simple conversations a struggle. I knew I had to clear the air with the people I cared about, explain my story, and prove my innocence.

But that meant facing some tough conversations that start in the same awkward place and never seem to go anywhere good. It wasn't something I looked forward to. Slowly, as I felt more comfortable being social again, I landed a good job in car sales. It wasn't easy, but I was taking it one step at a time, shedding that heavy suit, and learning to be social again. It was a step forward, a chance to rebuild my life, piece by piece.

Selling cars turned out to be a good fit. It played to my strengths, the kind of work I enjoyed that showcased my communication skills. The company was even a Fortune 100, which felt like a small victory after everything I'd been through. I ended up breaking the individual sales record that month and our team's sales figures were so high they probably wouldn't ever be touched.

Now, it wasn't all about us being sales superstars. Well, actually, we got lucky. Hurricane Harvey (2017) and Hurricane Imelda (2019) hit, and our car lot was fortunate enough to be located on high ground. My commute to work was clear, while others weren't so lucky. Many homes, including mine, were flooded. But when people need help, I always spring into action.

Helping people has always been a reflex for me. The minute the hurricane hit and the water started rising in my own house, I went into action mode. I immediately stripped out all the carpet, piled it up for disposal, sprayed bleach to prevent mold, and did everything necessary to clean it up. I managed to do all this before going to work. This determination helped me break the individual organic sales record.

But the real point wasn't the record. The real point was the people of southeast Texas. They lost their homes, their cars, everything. Their vehicles were their lifeline, their first step back to normalcy. And on a deep, personal level, I understood that. That feeling of needing to start over, to rebuild your life from the ground up.

Working with all those clients, thousands of them, started to chip away at the isolation I'd felt. People liked me again. I'm a people person, and I always have been. It felt good to connect, to counsel, to laugh, to have normal conversations, or for some to listen with an open heart to their terrible circumstances. For the first time in a long time, I felt like myself again. Almost.

There was still a part of me missing. There was still that lingering hesitancy, a constant scanning of the horizon, a side effect of the trauma I endured. I often felt hesitant and found myself looking over my shoulder. Like a soldier on edge even after the war is over. But slowly, piece by piece, I was putting myself back together.

This experience in car sales was challenging but incredibly rewarding. It highlighted my strengths and allowed me to connect with people on a very personal level.

Past my job in car sales, there's another important aspect of my life that I need to share: how I developed mental strength. This is the most crucial part of my story, and people often ask me, "How did you get through it all?" It's a big question with many answers. It wasn't easy, that's for sure. There were many pieces to the puzzle.

I learned many tools to handle stress during my time in the military. I focused hard on mental strength, anything I could do to stay centered. Meditation helped, and so did connecting with my faith. I'm a Christian, and reading the Bible for hours on end gave me a sense of perspective. It felt like those long passages offered hidden wisdom, messages that spoke directly to my soul in that dark time.

Calming my spirit wasn't enough, though. I also relied on the practical stress-reduction techniques I learned in the service, like breathing exercises, muscle tension, relaxation, distractions, and anything that could keep my mind from spiraling. And let me tell you, I had plenty of material to distract myself with. While I was there, I devoured over 500 books, most of them self-help. There wasn't much I didn't know about managing difficult situations by the time I got out. I even used the black and white writing books we are allowed to have featured 10-volume works cited containing things I thought most valuable out of each of the books, maybe to be used for self-reflection or even referencing a writing piece or even a book one day.

But of all the books I read, there's one that stood out at that time: "Man's Search for Meaning" by Viktor Frankl. It's a book I recommend to everyone, especially those lucky enough to never experience the kind of hardship I did. Frankl's story and his emphasis on finding meaning even in the darkest corners all resonated deeply with me. It became a beacon of hope, a reminder that the human spirit can endure even in the deepest depths of despair.

If you aren't familiar with Viktor Frankl, let me share his story. Viktor Frankl was an Austrian psychiatrist and neurologist who survived the horrors of the Holocaust. Born in 1905, he had a promising career in psychiatry before World War II. However, his life took a drastic turn when he and his family were deported to Nazi concentration camps in 1942.

Frankl endured unimaginable suffering during his time in the camps. He lost his wife, parents, and brother to the Holocaust. Despite the physical and emotional torture he faced, Frankl managed to find a profound sense of meaning in his suffering. This ability to find purpose amid extreme adversity became the foundation of his psychological theory, which he called logotherapy.

After the war, Frankl wrote about his experiences in the concentration camps in his book "Man's Search for Meaning." In it, he described how those who found meaning in their suffering were more likely to survive. He observed that even in the most brutal conditions, people could choose their attitudes and find purpose. Frankl believed that life has meaning under all circumstances, even the most miserable ones.

There is a quote from Viktor Frankl that I find particularly meaningful. He said, ***"When we are no longer able to change a situation, we are challenged to change ourselves."*** This idea resonated deeply with me. During my struggles, I couldn't change the external events, but I could change how I responded to them. This was a lesson taught to me by another Brig "book mentor," Dr. Stephen Covey, and his work on 'The 7 Habits of Highly Effective People' where he found that at our most basic level, to be successful, we must "mind the gap." It's a simple yet profound way of expressing that between any stimulus, there is a gap in time that allows us the opportunity to determine how we will react. Dr. Covey is another book mentor who taught me knowledge in such a way I eventually realized it made navigating the world a much easier place. I will recommend that he put out a lot of literature, and although it is a virtuous quest, it would probably take the average person many years to read it all. After all, I had plenty of time.

Apart from that, there was another fantastic quote by Frankl that has been stuck with me since the day I read it. It said,

"Live as if you were living already for the second time. As though you had acted wrongly the first time."

*– **Viktor Frankl***

This concept mirrored my own experience. While I couldn't erase the past, I could choose how I moved forward. I could use the lessons learned to become a better person and make a positive impact on the world. Frankl's story and teachings, along with Dr. Covey, have had a profound influence on my life. Their ability to break things down to find meaning in suffering mirrored my own experience. Their insights helped me understand that while I couldn't always control what happened to me, I could control how I responded. This lesson has been invaluable in building my mental strength and resilience.

The Bible, a book I'd always looked back on and cherished, became an anchor in the storm. It wasn't just about religious teachings but about finding comfort in familiar stories and wisdom that had resonated for centuries. Passages about perseverance and hope, even in the darkest times, felt like a lifeline thrown to me.

Reading the Bible wasn't a passive experience; it was a conversation. I grappled with the verses and searched for meaning that applied to my own situation. Sometimes, a particular line would jump out, offering solace or a new perspective. It was a source of strength that went beyond mere words; it was a feeling of connection to something bigger than myself.

The Bible wasn't just a source of comfort; it also instilled a sense of responsibility. The lessons of compassion, of fighting for what's right, resonated deeply. It fueled a fire within me, a determination to overcome my own struggles and advocate for those who couldn't speak for themselves.

The Bible and the clergy volunteers were my anchors, keeping me grounded through the most challenging times. If it weren't for the lessons I learned from them right out of the Bible, I wouldn't have understood things in the mature way I do now. Without the Bible and my support network, I honestly don't know if I would be here today to share my story.

One verse that stands out to me is from *Isaiah 41:10:* ***"So do not fear, for I am with you; do not be dismayed, for I am your God. I will strengthen you and help you; I will uphold you with my righteous right hand."*** This verse has given me immense comfort and strength.

The Bible and the support of those around me have been crucial at each stage of my journey. These elements have helped me endure and come out stronger on the other side. My faith and the wisdom from my book mentors and the Bible have been my guiding lights, helping me navigate life's toughest challenges.

Looking back, I realize that it wasn't any one thing that got me through. It was a combination of tools, a mental toolbox I'd built over the years. Meditation, faith, physical fitness, self-help books, the search for knowledge, and even the physical act of reading hundreds of them all played a part. But Frankl's message, the idea that we can find meaning even in suffering, was the spark that kept me going. It's a message that holds true not just for those facing unimaginable hardship but for anyone struggling in life. Even today, when the world seems chaotic and divided, I find strength in remembering that, and in a way, my world becomes whole again.

Transitioning from the challenges I faced in car sales and my journey toward mental strength, another significant aspect of my life was pursuing my dream of becoming a doctor. While working in car sales, I was also taking science classes, driven by my lifelong aspiration to enter the medical field. Despite having a Business Administration (B.B.A.) in technology management for job security, I had my sights set on becoming a doctor.

So, I enrolled in science courses, steadily working toward medical school. My efforts eventually paid off when I received acceptance into medical school. However, there were hurdles to overcome, particularly concerning licensing due to my background. I knew the risks and the potential roadblocks, but I was determined. Becoming a doctor wasn't just a dream anymore. It was a mission.

Putting off medical school was a tough decision, but the timing wasn't right. Now, years later, I'm finally enrolled again, from summer 2021 to the present. The future is still uncertain. There are licensing boards to navigate hurdles to overcome. They'll need to decide if my past disqualifies me, a decision that feels arbitrary at best.

Thankfully, most administrators I've spoken to haven't seen an issue. The worst feedback, and ironically the most inspiring, came from someone I deeply respect. They acknowledged the injustice of it all, the fact that no crime was committed. But they also reminded me of the American ideal - you do your time, you pay your debt, and then you move on. Those words stuck with me. Coming from someone I admired, they were a powerful motivator. They fueled the fire within me, the drive to keep pushing forward.

This life has a purpose for me, and I wouldn't let anything deter me from finding it. That determination, fueled by the support of others, became another weapon in my mental arsenal.

With medical school on hold, thanks to the flooded home hurricane rebuild and the COVID lockdowns, I found myself with a surprising amount of free time. Thankfully, by October of 2017, I'd completed my parole – all the tests, polygraphs, the whole gauntlet. I even had a letter of support from the head federal officer of the probation program.

This unexpected free time gave me a chance to revisit something I'd tried while in the brig: reaching out to people in power. Fueled by the belief that many policies are tested on the military first, a kind of trial run where lawsuits are off the table (it's called the Ferries Doctrine, and let me tell you, I'm a strong advocate for dismantling it, at least in certain areas), I contacted everyone I could think of. From Congress and oversight committees to individual representatives and even my local mayor, I bombarded them with messages. My search extended to non-profits and advocacy groups too, hoping to find someone who might be aware of the situation and its broader societal implications.

It all stemmed from a feeling of injustice. These policies, these trials on people like me – they had a ripple effect, impacting society as a whole. My parents had also tried reaching out to legislators on my behalf, but over time, their voices were lost in the shuffle.

Then came a surprising discovery. While I was locked away, others in my small hometown faced the same ordeal. In a place with a tiny population, the odds of it being a coincidence seemed impossibly low. Remembering my parents' earlier attempts, I contacted an organization called 'Save Our Heroes' and joined their team. We became advocates for people like me, working tirelessly to help them get back on their feet and rebuild their lives.

People would often ask me how I was doing so well after everything. My answer was always the same: keep your head down, be yourself, your authentic self. It may sound simple, but trust me, it's true. Just like in golf, keeping your head down through the swing keeps you out of trouble, out of the rough and the sand traps. And in life, it's the same principle.

Working with Save Our Heroes was a turning point. Connecting them with people in Washington who were facing similar problems felt like a small victory. We were a team united by a shared experience and a common goal: getting relief for those who were served injustice. There was a sense of companionship, a shared understanding that transcended words. We'd all been through the wringer, and now we were determined to help others avoid the same fate.

At first, things seemed promising. Many on the team started seeing results. It was a mixed bag, some joining for their own battles, others driven by a desire to help. However, as the organization gained momentum, achieving 501(c)(3) status and the ability to raise funds, a new reality loomed in front of us.

Unfortunately, I wasn't one of those who received relief during that push for justice. There were higher profile cases, flashier stories that seemed to grab attention more readily than mine, the ones that never quite fit the mold. The people I spoke to were confused. "What's really going on here?" they'd ask. "This seems political, not legal." And honestly, I couldn't disagree. There were no clear answers, just a frustrating sense of powerlessness. It felt like the system was rigged, the deck stacked against me, and even prepared with all of the facts and evidence today, I still do not know why they chose me to ruin — an aspiring, well-documented, and overly supported intelligence professional. Discouragement threatened to engulf me, but the faces of the other families I'd met kept me going.

The Obama administration had complete control at the time – the House, Senate, and the executive branch. It felt like they could do whatever they wanted, unchecked. They oversaw every government agency, and when you put the pieces together, it painted a bleak picture. But the human cost was the most heartbreaking part.

The pain inflicted on countless families was a pain I'd been intimately aware of since the beginning of this ordeal. It fueled my determination to keep fighting, to be a voice for those who couldn't speak for themselves. The injustice of it all burned a fire in my gut. Here I was, someone who had served my country, and now I felt like an outsider, ostracized by the very system I'd sworn to defend. It was a bitter pill to swallow, but it only strengthened my resolve. I wouldn't be silenced. My story deserved to be heard.

The experience wasn't a simple metamorphosis, like a caterpillar transforming into a butterfly. It was deeper than that, a fundamental shift in how I saw myself and the world around me. It wasn't just about growing up; it was about examining everything – my place in this vast yet strangely small world, the kind of impact I wanted to make.

This transformation stemmed from several influences. The leadership I received in the military played a role, as did the camaraderie with my fellow soldiers. But the most profound impact came from books. They became my companions, guiding me through the darkness and offering new perspectives.

My journey began with the Bible, a wellspring of wisdom and practical knowledge that helped me navigate the complexities of life. It was the foundation upon which I built my understanding of the world. From there, I devoured hundreds of books, each one adding a new layer to my already overly experienced worldview.

I can't share the entire list here, but there are a few that stand out. There's Viktor Frankl's "Man's Search for Meaning," a powerful reminder that we can find purpose even in the face of unimaginable hardship. Stephen Covey's "The 7 Habits of Highly Effective People" offered valuable lessons in leadership and personal growth. Simon Sinek's "Start With Why" challenged me to define my own core values and motivations.

These books, along with countless others, such as the biographies and autobiographies of each of our nation's founding fathers, became my teachers, shaping my character and propelling me forward. They weren't just words on a page but conversations guiding me toward a life filled with purpose and meaning. The search for that purpose continues, but with the knowledge I've gleaned from these influential works, I always feel empowered to make a positive difference in the world.

This knowledge, this burning desire to make a difference, intertwined with my advocacy efforts. It wasn't just about pursuing my own dreams anymore. It was about honoring the promises I'd made to those back in the brig. I vowed that when I got out, I wouldn't rest until I shared the story of our injustice with everyone who could help.

That promise fueled my persistence. It was the reason I kept pushing forward, becoming a more active advocate throughout graduate school, where I earned my Masters in Business Administration (MBA) with a focus on Marketing at the top of my class with nearly a 3.9 GPA and honors. Surprisingly, I was voted as the best team member as each module requires a team program of some sort, and evidently, I resonated well with everyone to earn that more personal and meaningful honor. This wasn't just an endeavor; it was a mission, a calling I couldn't ignore.

Chapter 7: Advocacy

"Injustice anywhere is a threat to justice everywhere."

Those words spoken by many great civil rights leaders in one way or another were delivered to me while reading a legal book that was about Dr. Martin Luther King Jr., who I will accredit for the quote that really sparked my fire for individual rights and the state of what I was observing and experiencing in our justice system. Looking back on how I became an advocate, it all began somewhere between talking to all of those incarcerated with me who shared a story similar to mine in the Brig and the information I was receiving from the work of my family when I returned home after serving my sentence. Despite feeling devastated, my father stood by me as my unwavering supporter, and to say the least, when I could get a complaint out about the facilities, I am not ashamed to say that my mother gave them hell.

My Dad instilled in me the strength to rise again and encouraged me to do whatever it took, saying, "This isn't the end! You must advocate for veterans' rights."

His determination and inspiration were inherited from my grandfather, who was also a passionate advocate for veterans. My family has long been members of the American Armed Forces, serving in every branch to a total that we have lost account for extending from his time serving in WWII; however, the number is well over twenty.

The spark for advocacy was ignited by my family's legacy, creating a passion within me that couldn't be dimmed. This passion was further fueled by a significant encounter with Bruce Lockett, a remarkable man who became more than a mentor; he became my guide in the world of advocacy. Bruce, a Marine Corps veteran and a dedicated Veteran Service Officer (VSO), took me under his wing and introduced me to the intricacies of advocating for veterans.

Although Bruce's passing was a profound loss, his impact on my life was immense. He opened my eyes to more complexities of veterans' issues that I hadn't fully understood during my time in service.

Learning from Bruce motivated me to do more. I wanted to raise my voice louder, to become a stronger advocate. This determination led me to engage with representatives, share my experiences, and advocate for meaningful policy changes benefiting veterans.

So, my journey into advocacy began because of the support and teaching of amazing people like my dad and Bruce Lockett. They supported and pushed me to make a real difference for veterans and their families. Reflecting on this journey fills me with gratitude for mentors like Bruce and the opportunity to impact veterans' lives positively. Advocacy isn't just a responsibility; it's a heartfelt commitment rooted in deep respect and duty toward those who have served our country.

Meeting Bruce was a life-changing experience. He wasn't just a pastor; he also played a crucial role in the Veteran Service Organization (VSO), which helped veterans. His dual roles as a spiritual guide and an advocate added depth to my journey. It was a sad day to watch him be given his honors, knowing that he wouldn't longer be able to assist others, but that only left a feeling inside that I personally must do more to fight for the rights of veterans.

Bruce taught me valuable skills and insights about being a Veteran Service Officer (VSO) and why it's important to help our veteran community. His wisdom and kindness helped shape how I approach advocacy and gave me a clear sense of purpose. A purpose that was not only led by the will to help others but also by the spirit to endure the struggle and giants I may face.

I also received incredible support from Randy Weber, the congressman, and his dedicated assistant. They went above and beyond to assist me and provide resources, making it easier for me to navigate the complexities of advocacy. While they had some limitations, they did an excellent job in their roles and made a big difference in helping veterans. Their dedication inspired me and showed me the power of working together to create positive changes. When I realized the 2008 and 2012 administrations were weaponizing the judicial system, I only dug in deeper because, at face value, the fight is bipartisan. Nobody wants to volunteer for war or send their family to an organization that wouldn't even recognize the nature of the events that occurred.

When I had the chance to meet with Randy Weber's office, it marked a crucial point in my journey as an advocate. Through that connection, I found myself at an exclusive event on a helipad in Beaumont, Texas, where Senator Ted Cruz made a historic announcement in front of a small crowd of fifty people. I was among the fortunate 50 people who witnessed this moment firsthand. It was a moment that felt timeless, a chance to be part of something bigger.

As a Veterans Advocate with plenty of information and stories to share, I knew I had limited time to make an impact. I focused on drawing attention to the issues within the military justice system that the media was highlighting. I spoke about specific cases caught in the mix and upcoming decisions that needed fair oversight. Being a firsthand witness to what was happening, I knew the importance of shedding light on these injustices and advocating for change.

This event marked my first step into advocacy on a public stage. While I had shared my story with a few people before, it often didn't get the attention it deserved. As an intelligence professional, it just felt normal, but I knew I needed to break from that mindset and connect with the audience more. That's when I realized that advocating in real-time, while events were unfolding, could have a more significant impact on helping others. This became my mission, and I shifted my focus to helping others who were facing similar challenges.

During my interaction with Senator Ted Cruz, I stressed the urgency of addressing issues within the military justice system. I made it clear that my aim wasn't just personal relief but broader reform benefiting many others. One case I brought up during that meeting was Eddie Gallagher, a decorated Navy SEAL of the time, to underscore the seriousness of the situation.

During our conversation, he expressed disbelief and concern, saying, "Nothing sounds right about that at all."

His genuine empathy prompted him to ask, "What can I do?"

It was then that I realized the power of sharing information and advocating for justice.

I explained to him the situation surrounding Eddie Gallagher, emphasizing that there seemed to be a lack of substantial evidence against him. I highlighted the recurring pattern of unfounded accusations targeting individuals like us, such as Gallagher.

In response, he took a proactive stance and offered his support to Gallagher. I believe his actions contributed to Gallagher's successful defense, as well as his family and legal team's support, resulting in the eventual freedom from legal entanglements.

Well, let me first give you an overview of Eddie's case. In 2018, a Navy SEAL named Eddie Gallagher became famous for allegations of serious crimes during his time in Mosul, Iraq, fighting against ISIS. Some of the accusations were about him stabbing a prisoner who couldn't defend themselves and targeting civilians as a sniper, resulting in at least two deaths. Despite being nominated for a prestigious Silver Star and praised as a great leader, Gallagher's case became very controversial.

You might have heard about Gallagher because President Trump and Fox News talked a lot about his case. Trump supported him publicly and mentioned a possible pardon before the trial, raising concerns about whether the trial could be fair due to possible outside influences.

During this chaotic time, a brave whistleblower from the SEAL community spoke out against what they saw as improper influence from higher-ups, emphasizing how important it is to maintain fairness and accountability in the military's legal system. Their actions showed a lot of courage in challenging norms and defending the system's integrity.

Gallagher, however, denied all the accusations and said he was not guilty. His defense argued that the death in question happened because of an airstrike, not because of what Gallagher did, and they suggested that the SEALs testifying against him were unhappy subordinates seeking revenge.

The case had a big twist when the judge unexpectedly let Gallagher go from custody, saying the prosecutors did something wrong. The main prosecutor was taken off the case after admitting to using software to track the defense team's communications, which violated Gallagher's rights.

Overall, the Gallagher case brought up complex issues about fairness in the military legal system, outside influences, and the bravery of those who speak up against what they see as unfairness.

That meeting with Senator Ted Cruz underscored the importance of raising awareness and rallying support for individuals facing unjust accusations, especially when Texas is always top tier in support, being number 1, 2, or 3 in recruiting for the Armed Forces year after year. It also demonstrated the impact that collective advocacy can have in ensuring fairness and accountability within our legal system.

Being part of that significant day, where political ambitions merged with advocacy for veterans' rights and justice, left a lasting impression on me. It strengthened my commitment to being a voice for the unheard and highlighted the impact advocacy can have in creating meaningful change.

Meeting Ted Cruz during that time held significant meaning for me. How I received his words, the Senator became an ally in my advocacy efforts, particularly in supporting Eddie Gallagher and the others I spoke of. After witnessing the positive outcome of Eddie Gallagher's case, I felt a glimmer of hope that perhaps we could continue making progress in advocating for justice.

However, despite my successes in helping others navigate legal challenges, I found myself still entangled in my own legal battles. It was frustrating to see progress for others while feeling stuck in my own situation.

One notable success I had was with former Florida Congressman, Army military officer, and West Point Graduate Allen West of Georgia, who later became the head of the Republican Party of Texas. In November 2019, I had the privilege of attending a meeting where LtCol Allen West spoke in person in my hometown. It was a unique experience because, through social media, I had previously engaged with his live events, where he discussed current issues and answered questions. So, in a way, we had already conversed before, and I greatly admired his ability to make sense of complex situations, something I also strive for.

I learned about LtCol Allen West's visit through an email while taking continuing education classes at Lamar University. Upon signing up and following the instructions, I found myself in a room listening to Mr. West, and it was truly worth the time. His speeches are captivating, and his life's history adds depth to his message.

During his talk, Mr. West shared insights into his life, his current endeavors, and his future plans. One topic of particular interest to me was that of Clint Lorance, someone I had been advocating for regarding veterans' rights.

I had the opportunity to speak with him about Clint Lorance's case. Clint had faced serious accusations after a tragic incident overseas, where he fired his weapon, resulting in someone's death. The authorities were quick to label it as murder, but Clint insisted he was following protocol. I sought Mr. West's advice on what more could be done to support Clint in his situation.

I explained to Allen the importance of upholding the principles of self-defense within the American legal system. I emphasized that individuals like Clint, who act in accordance with their training and duty, should not be unfairly punished. Alan listened attentively, and as he prepared to assume the position of Republican National Chairperson, he continued to share Clint's story, which led to a favorable resolution of a "full and unconditional" pardon, which had never been done before and Clint pursued a career in law where he now is has earned his Juris Doctorate of Law in hopes of practicing law.

Mr. West graciously shared information about the ongoing efforts to help Clint, and we exchanged ideas to ensure that all avenues of advocacy were explored thoroughly. It was a collaborative effort to ensure that Clint received the support he needed. Mr. West appreciated any additional insights or resources that could aid Clint's cause as I was more equipped to share information through my network in hopes of a positive outcome of justice.

Clint Lorance's journey through the justice system paints a picture of a man wronged by circumstances beyond his control. Despite the overwhelming evidence that exonerated him, he found himself unjustly imprisoned for over five years on charges of killing civilians. However, it became evident that the individuals he was accused of harming were actually bomb makers, as confirmed by fingerprint and DNA evidence. This is what we all signed up to do: find the bad guys and ensure they don't harm others through rigorous training and disciplined courses of action.

Clint's role in the incident was not one of direct action but rather a decision made to protect his fellow soldiers. When faced with a potential threat, he gave the order to fire in defense, a decision rooted in safeguarding his platoon's safety through a minefield. The subsequent portrayal of the riders as civilian casualties contradicted the reality of their involvement in creating improvised explosive devices, information that was withheld during the trial. Withholding information from the trial was not only a trend for war crimes but any and every case the prosecutors wanted to win. At this point, it is safe to say that the wins were not for the virtue of truth but for the sake of their own trumped-up pride, higher leadership, and the win.

Furthermore, critical evidence, such as an Army Report indicating the platoon was under surveillance for an impending attack, was not disclosed by the prosecution. The complex narrative woven around Clint's case highlighted the challenges and injustices faced by those serving in conflict zones. If this set a precedent, then everyone would be afraid to defend others and themselves, which would cripple our capabilities and will to support, defend, and fight.

Despite these tribulations, Clint Lorance persevered. Thanks to an advocacy campaign and the pardon issued by President Trump in 2019, he regained his freedom. Since then, he has dedicated himself to sharing his story through writing, with two books reflecting on his experience and offering insights into conservative activism.

Clint Lorance's journey ended with a day of justice, and now he has studied law to help people who can't speak up for themselves. He graduated from Appalachia School of Law and is taking the Oklahoma bar exam, but not without opposition, which is ok for free speech but a disgrace, all things considered. From my understanding, Clint wants to use his experiences to make sure the legal system is fair for everyone. With determination, he keeps moving forward, hoping his story helps make things better. Seeing how collective efforts can lead to positive changes is inspiring and shows that change is possible for those who need it. Much like Clint, this is all of our stories, with the exception of having assistance from those on high who really understand what was going on.

These experiences highlight the power of advocacy and the impact it can have on individuals' lives, especially in high-profile and significant cases. While I still faced personal challenges, seeing positive outcomes for others gave me renewed determination to continue fighting for justice and fairness.

During that same remarkable year, I had an amazing chance to meet Governor Abbott. A Former Orange County Republican Chairman in Southeast Texas and former service representative for Representative Steve Stockman Covey introduced us, setting the scene for Governor Abbott's inspiring speech about Texas progress. Every word he spoke filled me with immense pride for our state.

Our first meeting was equally impactful. While I planned to talk about fair treatment for veterans and suggest solutions to big problems, something powerful happened unexpectedly. As I shared my concerns with Governor Abbott, I felt compelled to pray for him and with him. It wasn't planned, but it felt right at that moment.

The time of us praying together truly captures the heart of that moment—a mix of advocacy, faith, and a shared commitment to progress. It was a symbolic moment for me before I headed to the Pentagon to seek support and push for change.

Since then, I've been actively reaching out to different people and organizations and sharing important information. Even though progress can be slow, it's important to see that it's happening, even if it's gradual. What matters most is that we're moving in the right direction, which shows positive change and improvements in addressing the issues I care about.

This experience has strengthened my belief in the power of advocacy, faith, and persistence. It's a reminder that small steps forward can lead to big results and contribute to a brighter future for veterans and our community.

When it came to my own case and injustice, I didn't just sit still. I advocated for a review and accountability in the military justice system by writing a letter to the members of the Defense Advisory Committee on Investigations, Prosecutions, and Defense of Sexual Assault in the Armed Forces (DAC-IPAD).

I have a vivid memory of the moment when I first learned about the Defense Advisory Committee during a Podcast featuring William Cassara J.D., a civilian defense attorney who was also my appellate defense attorney. As I listened, I learned of new pushes for policy changes that were taking shape and heard several words referencing people addressing the committee as victims, and I thought immediately, I am a victim, too. I wasn't the type that had traditionally spoken but was undoubtedly a victim, so I reached out to him to find out more. At some point, I learned that he was actually on the committee, and his passionate description of the committee's role in advocating for fairness and integrity in the armed forces filled me with hope and determination. Recognizing the importance of shedding light on overlooked aspects in similar cases, I reached out to Mr. Cassara to discuss the possibility of sharing my story with the committee. He wasn't sure how they would receive my request, but I was determined to find out if they would allow it. If not, it would be very telling that the committee was even more one-sided than we had thought before. I sent in my respectful request and waited. To my surprise, it was received better than I had expected. They plainly described the process and allowed me to publish documents and make public comments. This was the first time a victim of the agenda was finally going to have a voice, and it was me. Finally, a chance to share my story somewhere may have a much broader impact.

Having just found this open door of unprecedented opportunity, I reached out to several people I knew who could use this opportunity as well, Major Anderson, a former Airforce Major who not only shared my struggle and turned down a Presidential Pardon because it only restores rights without exoneration as innocent, and also was affiliated with a non-profit Save Our Hero's, an organization who's mission is focused on falsely accused service men and women in the military justice system. We were both actually featured on their pages while we were still in the Brig before I was fully aware of their true mission. He was surprised that such a thing was possible and submitted his request just as I had, which was also allowed.

One notable moment on the trip, once we were granted our requests, was that of Major Anderson's picking up a call from me to see where he was in his travels because we had to make it to either the Pentagon or Arlington, Virginia, his response speaks volumes to what this fight is really about; good and evil.

He said, "Darin, you are not going to believe this, but everything keeps getting in the way of my ability to make it; the enemy is fighting hard, Darin. I don't know if I am going to make it. The enemy doesn't want me, their man!" At that point, all I could do was do what I knew how to do. I told him he would make it and shrug the enemy off, and I would pray for his safe travels and arrival. He made it safe and in time, just as my dating partner of three years and I made the journey at that time.

The other person I reached out to was someone I met through advocacy who has been no less than instrumental in the continued progress being made, a Naval Academy Graduate from my hometown, Commander Owen's.

I must stop to say that my companion has also played an integral role in my journey. I was prepared to go alone, but she was adamant about coming with me and understanding more of what all of this was truly about after hearing me try to explain and tell more details as I learned more. I owe her a great debt of gratitude as I do not know of any woman I have ever had in my life strong enough to clearly see the flaws of the justice system, make such a long journey, and be so understanding about all of these things that happened to me, but also the bigger picture. I am certain the Good Lord brought her into my life for a reason, and for that reason, I am forever grateful.

In my own letter to the committee, I shared my background as a former Navy Intelligence Specialist who dedicated 12 years to serving my country with honor. I explained to the committee how my life took an unexpected turn when I was accused of sexual assault, resulting in a faulty guilty finding that greatly impacted my entire life in all aspects. I expressed the weight of injustice and my struggle for fairness, driven by a strong sense of duty and commitment to justice.

When given the opportunity to address the committee, I seized it. I advocated for creating a conviction integrity unit, proposing the establishment of the Armed Forces Falsely Accused Individual Review (FAIR) subcommittee. I argued that this subcommittee would ensure transparency, integrity, and accountability in cases involving Unlawful Command Influence (UCI) and rights violations.

During my presentation, I discussed the details of my case, focusing on UCI's pervasive influence and compromised rights for accused individuals. I emphasized how these flaws have affected the fairness of military justice, calling for a review process prioritizing truth and fairness for those who protect the very rights being violated.

In my plea to the committee, I not only sought personal exoneration but also aimed for broader changes in the military justice system. I urged for a review process free from external pressures and conflicts, emphasizing integrity, accountability, and respect for individual rights.

When the day of the meeting with DAC-IPAD arrived, a subcommittee of the Armed Forces Committee, I felt a mix of nervousness and conviction as I stood before the honorable members, not knowing if I was a lamb walking into the lion's den or would be received respectfully. I knew this was a crucial moment where I could make a meaningful impact. Speaking passionately, I emphasized the urgent need for a conviction integrity unit (FAIR subcommittee) to address injustices and protect the rights of service members. The most critical points at this meeting were that I was innocent, the armed forces have been shrugging off the largest occurrence of Unlawful Command Influence in military history, and I offered my research report of how this agenda began, was executed, affected all of our cases creating lawfare in the ranks, and the need for the integrity unit and other safeguards.

The atmosphere in the room was charged with discussions and debates, highlighting the gravity of the issues. This marked the beginning of my journey to advocate for reforms that would bring transparency, integrity, and accountability to the military justice system. I looked forward to upcoming meetings where I could delve deeper into these proposals and advocate for meaningful change.

However, I faced challenges along the way. Despite reaching out to many media outlets, I encountered resistance and reluctance to cover the story. Having been in the Intel community, I knew the news was all owned by the same people and was nothing much more than an echo chamber for whatever they wanted, but I would still try. External pressures posed obstacles, hindering the spread of crucial information and the urgency of reform. If it wasn't for the decentralization of information sharing, the military would likely never have faced public scrutiny because they had been trusted for so long by the majority of the population. We would later learn as a collective world that the reason speech wasn't reaching the right audiences was because all social media was being censored. This would be a defining moment in history where a single human being spent $44 billion dollars solely for the sake of free speech and exposing the reality we had been living: a life being programmed and altered by algorithms and bad actors.

Despite these challenges, my determination grew stronger. The passion to fight for justice and fairness in the military justice system fueled my efforts, and I remained committed to my mission of bringing about positive change.

Reflecting on those moments, I feel a profound sense of purpose and commitment. The road ahead may be tough, but I am prepared to face it head-on, knowing that each step brings us closer to a more just and equitable system for all service members and potentially a total reform of how the United States can treat the justice system more just.

Chapter 8: My Plight for Change

"The people who are crazy enough to think they can change the world are the ones who do."

– Steve Jobs

Although my plight is not to set out to change the world, every act of advocacy has the ability to change the world for even one person. However, where there is no path, and one must make a trail in this environment, it is likely that people will have problems with it and, to an extent, become opposed. Remembering a famous quote by former President Woodrow Wilson, "If you want to make enemies, try to change something." Obviously, I was never out to create any enemy or opposition, as my plight is bipartisan, yet he is inevitably correct in his timeless statement.

As I reflect on the twists and turns of my journey, advocating for a military free of sexual assault and striving for fair and impartial processes of justice, I find myself compelled to revisit a crucial chapter in my life. Having shared the details of my case, including the unjust conviction for sexual assault and the subsequent sentence to three years of confinement and a bad conduct discharge, I now stand at a point where I seek resolution and justice.

In the aftermath of the trial and my time behind bars, I had the opportunity to address the advisory committee on September 21, 2021. It was a moment where I poured my heart out through public comments, submitted documents, and shared my thoughts in the reading room. My purpose was clear—to highlight the injustice I endured and others had endured and why, and to finally bring to light among people who had to hear that I was wrongfully convicted.

In that discussion, I put forward a proposal for change. I introduced what I termed the Falsely Accused Individual Review (FAIR) unit, committee, or subcommittee. The essence of this entity would be to possess fact-finding authority, capable of making essential recommendations to the appellate services and/or board of corrections for adjudication. While my initial struggle focused on relief for those affected by Unlawful Command Influence, I strongly advocated for a permanent review committee in the interest of all service members and military justice.

This journey has been a rollercoaster of emotions—frustration, determination, and a deep sense of duty. Navigating a system that initially failed me demanded tenacity, yet with a glimmer of hope, I persisted. The Unlawful Command Influence, which none of my lawyers would submit for me, left me voiceless once again and unable to submit matters of my own, known as Grostefon matters. The blatant violations of human rights revealed through the mishandling of military court-martial over the past decade serve as stark reminders of the uphill battle for justice. It reminded me that even if I held the keys to justice in my own hands, they would do everything in their power to ensure it never saw the light of day.

At the court-martial, I carried the weight of the entire military justice system and its tainted ranks on my shoulders in that courtroom. Now, as I pen down these words, I carry the weight of a decade-long struggle but also the optimism that my story can contribute to a brighter future. The quest for justice is a winding road, but in sharing the details of my fight, I hope to inspire others to stand up against injustice and, together, champion a fair and just military system.

Now, turning the pages of my experiences, I feel compelled to shed light on a critical yet often overlooked aspect of my case: the implications of unlawful command influence (UCI) within the military justice system. As a victim of this issue, I find a sense of accountability to address it promptly, for the consequences of neglecting UCI can be profound.

The gravity of UCI cannot be overstated, as its unaddressed presence holds the potential for severe consequences within military justice proceedings and trust for new recruits and those serving throughout the services. UCI, being a form of bias, possesses the capacity to cast a shadow over the outcomes of court-martial cases. Given that commanders play a pivotal role in justice proceedings and wield discretion, particularly in recommending clemency, the risk of bias favoring military interests becomes apparent. This, in turn, can result in unfair and biased rulings.

The repercussions of inadequately addressing UCI extend beyond individual cases to have a lasting, negative impact on the military justice system and have spilled over into civilian courts, colleges, and other government courtrooms. This will undoubtedly leave negative precedents and ripples for the common American, but more specifically, as we have recently seen, it will weaponize for purely political purposes.

Soldiers, the very backbone of the system, have long begun harboring doubts about its fairness. Losing faith in commanders as impartial decision-makers has led to a breakdown of trust and morale. Additionally, this erosion of confidence has extended beyond the military ranks, affecting public perception of the military's disciplinary system.

These potential consequences underscore the urgency of addressing UCI comprehensively. It is not merely a matter of individual cases but a systemic challenge that, if left unattended, threatens the very foundation of not just military justice but justice in its entirety. As someone who has faced this intimately, I recognize the importance of highlighting these issues to ensure that the call for justice resonates beyond personal narratives, aiming for a systemic change that upholds the principles of fairness and impartiality.

To look into the reasons behind the issue, I've dedicated years to studying the subject and analyzing cases, drawing upon my own experiences to identify the most plausible changes and actions necessary to prevent others from enduring what I've faced.

As I reflect on this journey, a poignant observation came to light: One of the most significant problems lies not in the lack of knowledge regarding the issue or potential solutions but rather in the limited action taken to address it. The gap between awareness and implementation has persisted, underscoring the urgency for meaningful change. But who is in charge of that? Leadership and Congress. Both have the opportunity to stop their madness once it is heard or known of.

With a commitment to closing this gap, I've formulated thoughtful proposals aimed at addressing the core problem: Unlawful Command Influence (UCI). These proposed courses of action are designed not only to limit the occurrence of UCI but also to work toward the eradication of this detrimental influence. Additionally, there is a crucial focus on retroactively correcting wrongful convictions, acknowledging the gravity of the impact on those who have suffered unjustly, such as myself.

These proposals represent a bridge between identifying the problem and implementing effective solutions. Let me share with you the detailed proposals I've formulated after years of studying the subject and analyzing cases.

1. Strengthen enforcement of existing policies and regulations:

Recognizing that robust policies and regulations are already in place, the first step involves reinforcing their enforcement. Stricter adherence to existing guidelines will serve as a foundational measure in curbing instances of UCI. At the time of this writing, the committee has heard from many and has adopted some helpful insight for changes they have already made, but it is only one step in the right direction.

2. Implement an independent body for case reviews:

To instill a sense of impartiality and objectivity, there is a crucial need for an independent body within the military structure. This body would specialize in reviewing cases involving UCI, offering an unbiased perspective. Their role would extend beyond mere review, with the authority to make key corrective decisions, recommendations for disciplinary action, or propose changes to policies and regulations.

3. Enact stronger whistleblower protection:

Whistleblowers play a pivotal role in exposing instances of UCI, yet their actions often come with significant risks. To encourage a culture of transparency and accountability, stronger protections are essential. Enacting comprehensive whistleblower protection measures will shield those who report UCI, fostering an environment where individuals feel safe coming forward without fear of reprisals. I personally was reprised against, and the investigation led to a finding of true reprisal, but the person who was actually responsible could not be identified. Therefore, the only finding was recognition of reprisal. There is a list of reprisals against me and my efforts. However, that list is personal and may come out at another time.

4. Review cases of wrongful conviction:

It is imperative to revisit cases tainted by UCI broadly, acknowledging the inherent injustice. Establishing a dedicated effort to review such cases will allow for a thorough examination, ensuring fair treatment and due process. The focus will be on determining methods for providing restorative justice and offering redress to those who have been wrongfully convicted.

5. Create a task force for policy, procedure, and legislation review:

Recognizing the dynamic nature of military justice, a dedicated task force is essential. This body will undertake a comprehensive review of existing policies, procedures, and legislation, assessing their efficacy in preventing UCI. Any necessary changes will be identified and proposed to fortify protections against unlawful command influence.

6. Increase education and training:

Education is a cornerstone of prevention. By increasing military personnel's education and training, we empower individuals to recognize, report, and challenge instances of UCI. This proactive approach ensures that members of the military are well-equipped with the knowledge and tools needed to safeguard against undue influences. This means legitimate education and training, not unlawful commands, dear colleague letters, or propaganda campaigns, but real rules, legislation, and the like. I say this because, as we have all learned after congressional hearings, nobody gave the authority for the Title IX changes on college campuses or in the military. It was a select few who were able to rally others who didn't care about the rules, individual rights, and, most importantly, the US Constitution.

7. Establish a commission for ongoing recommendations:

To maintain a vigilant stance against UCI, a dedicated commission is essential. This body will continually assess the landscape, offering ongoing recommendations to protect military members from unlawful command influence. By fostering adaptability, this commission will play a pivotal role in ensuring the longevity and effectiveness of the proposed reforms. If the military implements the review of past cases stemming from the beginning of this all for those who make a UCI claim and ongoing recommendations to keep the true spirit of justice alive, then I have served my brothers and sisters well. This is my greatest dream.

These proposals, collectively woven into the fabric of military justice, represent a holistic approach to addressing UCI. Each element serves as a vital component in creating a system that is not only just and fair but also resilient to external influences that threaten its integrity. In my opinion, these proposals are as close to a perfect standard to guide us toward a future where justice prevails in the face of adversity as one can get.

In the relentless pursuit of justice, I've spent close to a decade fighting to clear my name. Unfortunately, the corrective actions needed to right the profound wrongs, not only for me but for fellow survivors of Unlawful Command Influence (UCI) in the Armed Forces, remain elusive.

As someone seeking justice, I pose a sincere question to those championing the cause of fairness: What would you do if you found yourself in my shoes, grappling with the realization that there seems to be no clear course of action for relief? It's a genuine inquiry, acknowledging that those on the committee possess a deeper understanding of the details of military justice, while I have learned from the inside out.

These pages serve the purpose of shedding light on my plight and drawing attention to my observation of an emerging correlation between rectifying injustice and revealing the embedded prejudice within the system.

In the world of military legal cases, the threat of unlawful command influence (UCI) still looms large, casting a shadow over justice. Yet, there are instances where courageous whistleblowers have stepped forward, shining a light on these wrongs. Their heroic deeds not only exposed misconduct but also emphasized the crucial values of transparency, integrity, and accountability within the military justice system.

I wish to highlight stories of courageous individuals whose endeavors have assisted justice in prevailing. These narratives embody the spirit of leadership necessary to combat the lingering effects of Unlawful Command Influence, which persist in disrupting careers and lives. Here are a few noteworthy cases that exemplify the bravery of these whistleblowers:

The commitment to justice and courage displayed by whistleblowers in cases like United States v. Barry is truly commendable. Rear Admiral Patrick J. Lorge and Captain David Wilson bravely stood up against unfair influence from high-ranking officials, even though it posed personal and professional risks. Their actions highlighted the importance of maintaining justice, regardless of one's rank.

In a similar act of courage, a Navy SEAL whistleblower in the United States v. Gallagher case challenged outside pressures that could have affected the trial of Chief Edward Gallagher for war crimes. Despite strong loyalty within the SEAL community, the whistleblower prioritized justice and accountability, emphasizing the need to uphold the military legal system's integrity.

Although I do not agree with his personal actions, in the United States v. Bergdahl case, whistleblowers brought attention to the dangers of unfair influence from President Trump's biased remarks during the trial. A military defense attorney bravely opposed the Commander-in-Chief's influence, stressing the importance of fair trials and judicial independence.

Lastly, in the case of US v. Gilmet, whistleblowers faced a tough decision when exposing a Lieutenant Colonel's misconduct and abuse of power. Despite potential career risks and threats of retaliation, these individuals remained dedicated to justice and military integrity, serving as inspirations for others to follow.

The heroism displayed by these whistleblowers in military legal cases cannot be overstated. While some stories may stem from acts of bullying or cowardice, the virtuous actions of whistleblowers ultimately emerge, embodying courage, integrity, and a profound sense of responsibility. By fearlessly exposing unlawful command influence, they play a crucial role in ensuring that justice prevails.

Their actions set a powerful precedent for transparency, fairness, and accountability within the military justice system. It is paramount to recognize, protect, and celebrate these whistleblowers, as their bravery contributes significantly to the ongoing enhancement of the military legal system.

While the specifics of these cases may differ, the root problem remains the same: UCI. Through these stories, I aspire to inspire those who hold the key to simple testimonies that could potentially result in someone's freedom, the clearing of a name, and the hopeful return to a somewhat normal life, considering all the challenges faced.

These examples underscore the pivotal role of whistleblowers in preserving the principles of justice within the military. Their actions stand as beacons of integrity, guiding others to follow suit in the pursuit of a just and transparent military legal system.

Chapter 9: The Good, The Bad, The Ugly

"We must always take sides. Neutrality helps the oppressor, never the victim. Silence encourages the tormentor, never the tormented."

– Elie Wiesel, Holocaust Survivor

As I continue my pursuit of justice, Elie's words resonate deeply: take a side, but choose the side of truth. Take control as the victim, and don't let the system define you. Silence the tormentors with truth and facts, striving to break free from the cycle of torment. Without these guiding principles, change—especially positive change—would remain just a distant dream, like a child's vision of a carefree life.

Now, personally, I've witnessed a mix of positive changes, persistent challenges, and the sheer ugliness of the obstacles I've faced. The road ahead has not been an easy one, but I remain steadfast in my determination to see this through.

On the positive side, I have seen glimmers of hope as the tide slowly turns. The opportunity to address the Defense Advisory Committee on Investigations, Prosecutions, and Defense of Sexual Assault in the Armed Forces (DAC-IPAD) was a significant milestone. Being the first victim of Unlawful Command Influence (UCI) to do so was a profound moment. It signaled a potential shift in the willingness to confront this systemic issue.

The committee's receptiveness to my proposal for a Falsely Accused Individual Review (FAIR) unit was encouraging. This proposed subcommittee could be the key to providing much-needed transparency, integrity, and accountability within the military justice system. If implemented, it would offer a glimmer of hope for those wrongfully accused, like myself, to seek redress and clear their names.

However, the negative aspects of this journey have been equally persistent. The reluctance of media outlets to cover these stories, despite my best efforts, has been a frustrating barrier. It's as if there is a concerted effort to keep these injustices hidden from public view, perpetuating the cycle of silence and indifference.

The psychological warfare waged within the brig has also been a constant thorn in my side. The tactics of the 'Goon Squad,' including harassment, intimidation, and blatant disregard for our rights, have been harrowing experiences. The fact that our complaints were dismissed or brushed aside only fueled the sense of hopelessness and the realization that the system was rigged against us. Oddly, some law enforcement outside of the brig chose to carry on this "goon" mentality, which to this day still does not settle well. It's nearly much like a game of chance; it depends on who you are assigned to or who takes an ill-intended and unnecessary interest in you for whatever reason.

The mistreatment by the medical staff, who seemed more intent on inflicting further punishment than providing care, has been particularly gut-wrenching. Their callous disregard for our well-being and the lack of accountability only deepened the sense of betrayal by those who were supposed to uphold the principles of justice and rehabilitation.

In addition, military recruiting is increasingly becoming a struggle as the population's trust in the armed forces has eroded over time. Given the opportunity to make things right, rather than restoring this trust through reforms and transparency, the government has instead resorted to implementing a draft. The House version of the National Defense Authorization Act (NDAA), passed last month, mandates automatic registration for all men. Now, a new Senate version seeks to expand this requirement to include women, signaling a significant shift in military policy amidst growing public disillusionment.

As I continue to pursue my path, these broader changes serve as both a backdrop and a source of reflection on the nature of justice and systemic reform. In the wider landscape of defense and government policy, recent developments reflect both progress and ongoing debates:

1. Senate Armed Services Committee Proposal:

The Senate Armed Services Committee's version of the defense policy bill includes a proposal to make military conscription registration automatic for all citizens between the ages of 18 and 26, extending this requirement to women. Chairman Sen. Jack Reed (D-R.I.) has championed this change, which is now set for debate on the Senate floor. This proposal represents a significant shift in military policy, aiming to broaden the pool of registered individuals for conscription.

2. Cyber Services Procurement:

The 2025 defense policy bill suggests altering the 2022 provision on cyber services procurement. The amendment would allow Department of Defense (DoD) components to purchase cyber services independently if they can demonstrate a compelling need or ensure market competition. This diverges from the previous requirement for centralized procurement.

3. General Services Administration (GSA) Funding Request:

The GSA has requested $425 million in the upcoming budget to optimize and offload unneeded office space. This funding aims to address missed opportunities for consolidation and cost-saving over the past eight years, underscoring the need for strategic space management.

4. Veterans Benefits Administration (VBA) Overtime Policy:

The VBA is shifting from mandatory to mostly voluntary overtime, capping it at 20 hours per month. This change, driven by Under Secretary Joshua Jacobs, seeks to address unsustainable practices and improve employee work-life balance.

5. U.S. Citizenship and Immigration Services (USCIS) Staffing and Morale:

Despite staffing challenges and funding limitations, USCIS has seen an increase in employee engagement. The agency's score in the Best Places to Work rankings has risen, reflecting efforts to support the workforce through town halls and improved supervisor training.

6. Environmental Protection Agency (EPA) Union Contract:

The EPA and the American Federation of Government Employees have signed a new collective bargaining agreement covering 8,000 staff members. The contract includes provisions on diversity, equity, inclusion, accessibility, and scientific integrity.

7. Department of Homeland Security (DHS) Staffing and AI Recruitment:

DHS's Countering Weapons of Mass Destruction Office is rebuilding its workforce after concerns about attrition. The department is also recruiting 20 additional experts for its Artificial Intelligence Corps. These hires will focus on AI applications, oversight, and policy development.

These updates illustrate the ongoing evolution of defense and government policies, reflecting both advancements and areas needing attention. If these problems are not addressed now, we risk making a mess of our military and undermining the very structures we rely on. This could lead to a cycle that creates more "alleged" victims. If history repeats itself, it may turn into a scam for individuals who don't want to serve. They could make claims to avoid service, secure choice orders, and receive benefits while others struggle for the rest of their lives.

Despite these challenges, I have remained steadfast in my advocacy efforts. The meetings, speeches, and letters I've written to raise awareness and demand change have been crucial to this journey. By sharing my story and the stories of others, I aim to chip away at the wall of silence and indifference. My hope is to inspire others to join the fight for justice.

Throughout it all, I have sought ways to protect myself and stay focused. Immersing myself in my faith, reading, and education has been a lifeline. This has allowed me to expand my knowledge and find solace in the wisdom of those who have overcome adversity. It stands as a testament to the power of the human spirit to persevere, even in the face of daunting obstacles.

Chapter 10: Military Justice and the Challenges Ahead

"Our lives begin to end the day we become silent about things that matter."

– Dr. Martin Luther King

As I've navigated this complex and often frustrating journey surrounding military justice and life after trauma, I've had the opportunity to interact with high-ranking officials. These include members of Congress, state and local leaders, powerful attorneys, and military officials who genuinely want to hear me out. These interactions have been a mixed bag. Some have offered glimmers of hope, while others have reinforced the systemic challenges that continue to plague the military justice system. In reflection, I realized that the most powerful weapon that can be formed against such corruption and downright evil is the people. Good people who care are brave enough to speak their truth and have the endurance to never quit.

My meeting with Senator Ted Cruz was a particularly significant moment. His genuine concern and willingness to potentially offer support for individuals like Eddie Gallagher and Keith Barry demonstrated the power of advocacy and the potential for change when influential figures are willing to lend their voice, whether public or behind closed doors. This experience underscored the importance of building relationships with those in power. It highlighted the need to leverage their influence to drive meaningful reform. In short, positive changes have come from good people. Period. Every positive movement toward progress has come from heroic souls with integrity and bravery. Those who lack these qualities remain stuck, much like crabs in a bucket. They often struggle to make things happen, but they do find ways to push through out of necessity. They don the armor of God and leadership to accomplish a better system and, ultimately, a better quality of life. Again, it's all about the people. When people change, policies will follow.

However, my encounters with the Inspector General have been quite different. Discovering that the hotline for reporting issues within the brig was nothing more than a facade was shocking. It laid bare the extent to which the system was rigged against us, with no legitimate avenues for seeking redress or accountability. Even when trying to submit Grostefan matters—issues you submit on your own when lawyers refuse to follow your orders—there are obstacles. This occurs whether they are sworn to protect you by military order or if you pay a civilian attorney. If the information is damning to the service, they often stop short and deny my ability to have my own voice. Their voice was the only ones that mattered evidently, even though, at this point, for a retrial, that information is absolutely necessary. So without conspiracy, they are all well versed in law, enough not to prolong hearings if the individual runs out of money and the evidence gets them a new trial.

The psychological warfare waged within the brig was equally disturbing. The constant threats, harassment, and blatant disregard for our rights were a testament to the dehumanizing nature of the environment we were forced to endure. The "Goon Squad" and their tactics of intimidation were a constant reminder of the power imbalance and the lengths to which the authorities were willing to go to maintain control.

The mistreatment by the medical staff was particularly egregious. Their seeming indifference to our well-being and the lack of proper medical care only compounded the physical and emotional toll of our incarceration. This was a stark reminder that the system was not designed to rehabilitate or support us; it was meant to punish and break us.

Throughout this ordeal, I've learned the importance of speaking up and advocating for change within the system. The letters I've written, the meetings I've attended, and the connections I've made have all been part of a broader effort to raise awareness and drive meaningful reform. It's been a challenging and often frustrating process, but I remain committed to being a voice for those who have been silenced and a catalyst for the transformation of the military justice system.

In the face of these challenges, I've also found solace in immersing myself in reading and education. The works of Viktor Frankl, Stephen Covey, John Maxwell, and others, such as my spiritual leaders of that time, have provided me with the tools and the inspiration to navigate this difficult journey. By cultivating a deeper understanding of the human experience and the power of resilience, I've been able to stay focused and maintain a sense of purpose, even in the darkest of times.

As I look to the future, I remain steadfast in my belief that the tide can be turned and that justice can prevail. The measures I've taken to protect myself and stay focused, coupled with my unwavering commitment to advocacy and reform, have been instrumental in sustaining me through this arduous process. I am determined to continue fighting, to be a beacon of hope for those who have been wronged, and to contribute to the creation of a new age of military justice that is truly fair, transparent, and accountable.

Unfortunately, according to the most recent meetings of the Defense Advisory Committee responsible for this topic (DAC-IPAD), even though we bring them the bad and the ugly, hoping to find some resolve, they stick to topics such as the following:

DAC-IPAD Key Problems Identified:

1. Racial and Ethnic Disparities: The reports indicate concerns about racial and ethnic disparities in the investigation, prosecution, and conviction of sexual offenses in the military.

This, of course, is a problem that needed to be addressed probably around the time the UCNL was crafted but had not been, which, in my opinion, is disgusting for a first world.

2. Victim Access to Information: Issues have been identified regarding victims' access to information about their cases.

3. Pretrial Procedures and Prosecution Standards: The reports suggest a need for reforming pretrial procedures and establishing uniform prosecution standards.

4. Victim Impact Statements: The committee is examining the use and impact of victim impact statements in the military justice system.

5. Collateral Misconduct: The reports indicate a need to assess the issue of collateral misconduct and its impact on victims (note how it doesn't say falsely accused victims).

As anyone can clearly see, their problematic agenda is still victim-centric. It's almost as if they don't know what a victim is anymore. Yes, many will have merit, but what we deliver is ACTUAL REAL TIME IDENTIFIED PROBLEMS! One I know very well is MINE! No evidence, nobody believes it, and everyone criticizes the court's work, yet still no justice.

At this point, we have made great strides to have wave after wave of wrongfully accused testify, yet this is still their aim. Victims. This is ironic because they are creating more victims than assisting actual victims, in my opinion. Also, the data is impossible to find according to the services and Government Accountability Office (GAO), and those others with oversight or record-keeping capability will tell you it doesn't exist. Now let's look at what possible solutions could be proposed:

DAC-IPAD Possible Solutions:

1. Conviction Integrity Units: The committee is exploring the feasibility and advisability of establishing conviction integrity units to review potential wrongful convictions.

2. Uniform Policy for Sharing Information with Victims: The committee has made recommendations for a uniform policy to improve information sharing with victims and their counsel.

3. Randomizing Court-Martial Panel Member Selection: The committee has looked at the possibility of randomizing the selection of court-martial panel members to enhance fairness.

4. Reforming Pretrial Procedures and Establishing Uniform Prosecution Standards: The committee has provided recommendations for reforms in this area.

5. Improving the Special Victims' Counsel/Victims' Legal Counsel Programs: The reports suggest examining tour lengths and rating chain structures for these programs.

The only valid concern here, which causes the most damage, is that while conviction integrity units were a valuable step forward, they ultimately fell short. I believe I helped pioneer them. Randomized Court-Martial panels will help some, but when it comes to a man or woman of color who is an officer, they will be judged by their peers, who are majority white officers, given the nature of the commissioning programs. However, as you will see, when this all started, things became difficult. Victims were, for some reason, protected better than the Federal Reserve, even though they weren't truly victims yet; they were 'alleged victims.' Meanwhile, we had no support. What support we did have was far below par, for whatever reason—be it willful negligence or something else. Yet again, there was a focus on a single type of victim rather than addressing victims from both sides of the aisle that they created. Now that we have touched upon the Advisory Committee's plans and apparent lack of presence and consciousness, they appear to be doing what their representatives tell them to most of the meetings. So again, it's a people problem. It stems from Congress not doing things right. High-ranking officials who chose self-preservation over doing the right thing could have been whistle-blowers who were cowards. But let's look at the potential impacts on the armed forces, especially since all of this has been occurring for fifteen years:

Impacts on the Armed Forces and their Capabilities:

The work of the DAC-IPAD is likely to have a **significant** effect on the military justice system, particularly in the handling of sexual assault cases. *The committee's recommendations and findings could lead to policy changes, legislative reforms, and improved practices within the Armed Forces.* Key areas of impact may include:

1. Enhanced fairness and transparency in the military justice process.

2. Improved support and access to information for victims of sexual assault.

3. Addressing racial and ethnic disparities in the investigation, prosecution, and conviction of sexual offenses.

4. Strengthening the Special Victims' Counsel/Victims' Legal Counsel programs.

5. Promoting a more consistent and effective approach to pretrial procedures and prosecution standards.

Overall, the work of the DAC-IPAD aims to ensure that the military justice system effectively addresses sexual assault cases. It seeks to uphold the rights and interests of both victims and the accused. The implementation of the committee's recommendations could contribute to a more just and equitable military justice system.

As you just read, none of their current agenda has anything to do with both the accused and the victim. Not even the 100 people we've had reach out as victims, and the thousands that we know of won't speak out. That is the problem: a hammer only sees nails. When the hammer has no light around it and feels it's time to hammer, it won't always hit a nail; sometimes, it will crush and break a hand instead.

So even after all that work, years of investigation, advocacy, and progress, the Defense Advisory Committee is still stacking its agenda against an accused even though they have been working on this since 2010.

In closing, I want to keep this simple: it's about people. Remember those "people" I mentioned who are so important? That person is now YOU. The ball is in your court, and you have every right to question authority about what's been going on. If you're inspired to be one of those people who do good deeds after reading this, consider writing a letter, making a phone call, or advocating to your local congressperson. Bring them a copy of my book and share your thoughts from the heart. Ask them to be more active with DAC-IPAD issues because they are not addressing victims' concerns. They are addressing "victim" concerns, not the wrongfully accused and convicted. If this doesn't get corrected now, it WILL only get worse before it may, if it ever gets better.

The reason is that " The work of the DAC-IPAD aims to ensure that the military justice system effectively addresses sexual assault cases while upholding the rights of both victims and the accused. The implementation of the committee's recommendations could contribute to a more just and equitable military justice system." – DAC-IPAD.

They do have the power to make recommendations as they investigate issues related to sexual assault, which should support both victims and the accused; however, right now, the focus seems heavily on protecting 'alleged victims,' and we can only know the truth after the evidence is thoroughly examined.

The most challenging aspect of this situation is that the Defense Advisory Committee on the Investigation, Prosecution, and Defense of Sexual Assault in the Armed Forces (DAC-IPAD) makes crucial recommendations. However, the responsibility for implementing these recommendations falls primarily on the Department of Defense (DoD) and Congress. This implementation faces significant hurdles because the DoD is partially responsible for the current failures in the justice system. Congress, often seen as the instigator of this invisible war, has staged events to influence funding decisions. One notable instance was when Michelle Obama designated April 2010 as Sexual Assault Awareness Month.

This situation reflects a psychological operation against our own troops. Meanwhile, the Department of Education lacks the authority to enforce meaningful laws or regulations. This is why college students have had more success in seeking justice; they can file lawsuits, and most of them have won. Unfortunately, you cannot sue the military in the same way you can sue a federally funded college.

The consequences of these systemic failures are dire. Innocent people have lost their lives. Some committed suicide after facing mere allegations, only to be found innocent later in court. Others couldn't handle the immense stress and took their own lives in various ways. I have witnessed individuals attempting to hang themselves or seriously injuring themselves. Some consumed handfuls of prescription pills in a desperate attempt to escape the nightmare imposed on them by the government and those involved in their cases.

There are many unscrupulous individuals trying to manipulate people—possibly even you—into doing their bidding. Thankfully, we are beginning to expose these unlawful command influences; otherwise, many would still be trapped in despair without hope.

As you stand before Congress, remember that you are speaking not just for yourself but for every innocent soul wrongfully burdened with guilt. Your voice matters more than you may realize, and your inquiries through the DAC-IPAD can help amplify the efforts to free the innocent. You have the power to question, challenge, and reshape the process.

Make sure to ask the tough questions, demand transparency, and refuse to accept half-measures. Write directly to DAC-IPAD, submit your concerns, and share your thoughts. Let them know we demand a military justice system that is truly just. This is your opportunity to advocate for change with respect and determination.

The committee isn't the enemy; they are limited in what they can do until Congress and the DoD decide to listen to the experts instead of their own narrow perspectives. It's time to stop being overlooked. This is not a partisan issue; it is fundamentally about justice. The military justice system should not drag the accused into the public arena, forcing them to prove their innocence. We need reform, and we need it now.

The time to act is now. Visit the following links to learn more and take your first steps towards change:

- DAC-IPAD Website: https://dacipad.whs.mil/

- Darin Lopez's Website: https://darinlopez.com/

And here's the challenge for you: write to DAC-IPAD today, email Congress, share your story, speak out for those who are voiceless and trapped in a broken system, and demand a military justice system that serves the true spirit of justice—not the interests of a flawed process.

Take Action Now

Email the White House here: president@whitehouse.gov to urge the government to prioritize military justice reform. Make your voice heard. Together, we can push for a system that upholds fairness and integrity for both the accused and the accuser.